D1472862

Edward Charles Elliott, Educator

Edward Charles Elliott, Educator

by Frank K. Burrin

Purdue University Studies

Lafayette, Indiana

1970

© 1970 by Purdue Research Foundation
Library of Congress Catalog No. 69-11274
International Standard Book Number 0-911198-19-9
Printed in United States of America

As president of Purdue I will not consider that I have met my responsibilities until the leadership and citizenship of the state of Indiana, of whatever class or occupation, continue to recognize that this University is their University; that Purdue University is an integral part of the public school system of the State ever working in its own distinctive and assigned fields; that Purdue is a worthy agency, ever at their disposal for aiding them to meet the needs that determine the happiness, the satisfaction and the ideals of their lives; until there is firmly established among students and teachers and alumni the enduring principle that the daily work of men makes education possible, and that education in turn must make the daily work of men possible and pleasurable.

Edward C. Elliott

1922

Contents

Author's Foreword

Edward Charles Elliott was elected sixth president of Purdue University on May 16, 1922. Born in 1874, the same year Purdue opened its doors to students, he had spent twenty-three years as a high school teacher, school superintendent, university professor, and chancellor of a state system for higher education. Forty-seven years old and halfway through his professional career, Elliott spent the next twenty-three years as Purdue's president.

In many ways his career at Purdue University was the culmination of his previous twenty-three years in education, for it enabled him to work as never before toward his personal goal: to discover and develop individuals of superior ability and to send them on to take part in the work of the world.

On the other hand, his pioneering scholarly activities in the areas of teacher training, school surveys, measuring teacher competency, and the grading of school work had already accorded him a prominent place among the educators of the nation. Thus his early work in the field of education together with his strong, sometimes brilliant, leadership as an administrator and consultant in higher education has mandated a careful review of his professional work. By any standards, Elliott had no small part in the development of American education during the first half of the century.

Any attempt to tell the story of Elliott at Purdue requires a review of his lifetime if a proper perspective is to be maintained. This account is, in part, a biography, although not a record of his personal life; it is, in part, an historical record of the institutions which he served (with particular reference to Purdue University) although not the complete story by any means; and finally, to a certain extent, it relates his career to the historical development of education in America during the period 1900-1950, and the issues faced by American educators during those years.

I first met Elliott in the spring of 1952, seven years after he had retired as president of Purdue. Robert Johns, then assistant to Purdue's seventh president, Frederick L. Hovde, introduced me as the graduate research fellow who had been selected to make a detailed study of the papers and works of Elliott. Johns, along with G. Stanley Meikle, then vice president of the Purdue Research Foundation, and B. L. Dodds, then director of the Division of Education and Applied Psychology, had approached Elliott earlier and had received his approval and support of the project. Thirty minutes later the three of us had agreed that work on the dissertation would begin July 1, 1952.

During the next two years I shared his office, using his personal papers and files with absolute freedom, and asking hundreds of personal and impersonal questions which were answered in every instance. His complete cooperation and willingness to devote many hours to this work was a rich experience for me. His patience and consideration, while certainly understandable, went beyond what might have been and made the association a thoroughly delightful one.

Elliott was very reluctant, however, to discuss any matters relating to his own family. "This dissertation is not a biography," he said on several occasions; and I did not visit him in his home until after the death of Mrs. Elliott. It was not until several years after his death that I met his brother, Benjamin, and his sons, John and Edward.

One morning when I came to "our" office, I found several pages which he had written for me headed, "The Personal Framework." "It is self-evident that the working enterprises of a lifetime are carried on and determined within a personal structure," he had noted, but he had gone ahead to provide only a sketchy outline of dates and events of a personal nature. We later agreed that the influence of specific individuals or certain personal events on the course of a career is at best difficult to determine; and once determined, even more difficult to place in balance.

When we talked about his professional relationships with his colleagues and associates, however, it seemed that he welcomed the opportunity to talk about people and places and events. Without question, his primary interests in life centered about his professional work rather than home and family. Although his family meant a great deal to him, he seemed to be always on a "work binge" and family vacations, for example, were rare events.

Most of his so-called "extra curricular activities" really weren't, because they usually involved, in one way or another, professional people with whom he worked.

Throughout all of our discussions Elliott kept bringing up what he called "the doctrine of chance." His own review of his professional years would have placed a major emphasis upon time and place as the major determinants in a career. "Chance meetings, unexpected conversations, all play a more important part in an individual's life than do most planned and carefully executed experiences," he often reiterated. "Pure chance determines a life work."

When I pointed out that there were always other elements involved in decision making, he invariably came back with examples to "prove" his point: "Chance took me to Leadville, Colorado, instead of Omaha in 1897," he said; "A chance acquaintanceship with a student at the University of Wisconsin led to my moving to Montana; an unusually hot night in Illinois—you could hear the corn cracking in the fields—led me to accept a position in Madison (Wisconsin) rather than Urbana," he continued. "The critical things in life happen without prevision, or are sheer accidents."

I did not accept this point of view, however, because it seemed clear that more often than not, significant events in his life followed a perfectly logical sequence and were generally the results of his own interests and energies. Neither did the dissertation on which this book is based subscribe to his "doctrine of chance."

The primary source of materials was Elliott's collection of his papers and addresses. The collection, which dates from 1891, includes manuscripts, typed and mimeographed material, printed papers taken from the original publication, books, reports, letters, and press clippings. Of great value, of course, was the opportunity for extended conversations with Elliott; but there have been many other conversations with people who knew Elliott, worked with him, or had simply observed him in action. The anecdotes about this man are legion.

In addition, the Purdue Libraries have retained a copy of each of Elliott's books and each of his separately bound reports as well as a collection of letters which were on file in his office. This together with Elliott's scrapbooks of press clippings and photographs now belongs to Purdue University. A selected bibliography of Elliott's works appears as an appendix to this volume.

When Elliott retired from Purdue on June 30, 1945, however, he removed from his office various personal items, a selected letter file, along with certain photographs and a memorial album and placed these in storage in a local warehouse. Also stored at this time were many items and furnishings from the Elliott home. A disastrous fire leveled the warehouse later that year destroying hundreds of letters, papers, and articles of inestimable value to the Elliott family. The loss did not affect the study of Elliott's professional career to a great extent, but it did limit the search for personal information.

For their help and encouragement I gratefully acknowledge my indebtedness to President Frederick L. Hovde; Paul Alexander, dean of education; M. B. Ogle, dean of the School of Humanities, Social Science, and Education; J. H. Moriarty, director of libraries; and William J. Whalen, university editor, all of Purdue University. And there were many others, some of whom are mentioned from time to time in the text, who were most helpful. Special thanks, of course, go to John and Ed Elliott and other members of the family, as well as members of my own family.

It has seemed appropriate to us to publish this record of Elliott's contributions to the nation because to review his career is to review many of the problems and issues which continue to face educators and educational institutions. When Elliott compiled a volume of selected papers of President Nicholas Murray Butler (of Columbia University) in 1936, he wrote a line which perhaps is applicable for use in connection with this book: ". . . this material conserves some of the best of the experience and some of the wisest of interpretation of American education and American life . . . ."

Frank K. Burrin

Lafayette, Indiana
January 1969

Introduction

In a real sense, I watched this biography being written by its then young author, Frank K. Burrin, who had chosen to write his thesis for his advanced degree about the life and work of one of America's outstanding administrators in the field of publicly-supported higher education.

Frank Burrin had what few biographers have when they work—namely, almost daily consultation with the man himself over a period of several years to check and recheck every facet and fact of his story.

Edward Charles Elliott became president of Purdue University in the early years of the decade known as the "Roaring Twenties," a period of tremendous growth in the nation's publicly-supported universities, and served his institution through the period of severe national trial known as the Great Depression, through the nation's economic recovery during the late thirties, and then into the cataclysmic years of World War II.

In the years of his tenure as president, major social, economic, and political upheavals and crises had direct and profound effects on universities and their basic missions of advanced teaching, research, and extension education, as they do today.

In good times and bad throughout his twenty-three-year tenure, Purdue University flourished in a dynamic way, because the most descriptive word for the man himself is dynamic.

I knew him as an engaging, yet powerful personality—certainly a strong-minded individual who could meet and hold his own with any man.

At all times he was an individual like no one else, and he tackled his problems in his own inimitable way. He set humanity above administrative regulation. He viewed people and their problems in their individual setting, and he vigorously resisted classifying all problems in terms of ancient ordinances and practices.

President Elliott's leadership was by no means confined to Purdue University alone. During his time as a university president, he was indeed one of the acknowledged leaders in the hierarchy of educators in this country.

In 1938 President Elliott was the motivating individual who called together a group of thirteen university presidents from leading public and private institutions in the Midwest. When this group, which called itself the Committee of Thirteen, met that year in Chicago, he was elected chairman, and he served in that capacity until his retirement from Purdue in 1945. This group met regularly and later became what is known today as the Council of Ten—the presidents of the universities in the Intercollegiate Conference of Faculty Representatives, commonly called the Big Ten.

It was typical of President Elliott, in his early leadership of this organization devoted to initiation and sponsorship of interuniversity cooperative endeavors, that he insisted upon institutional individuality. The meetings themselves were to be informal discussions where presidents could speak freely. They were to be confidential and afford an opportunity for frank discussion without the worry of premature publicity. "And," said President Elliott, "if the president of the institution is not interested or cannot attend, don't send a substitute!"

Until his retirement, President Elliott missed but one meeting of this committee—a remarkable testimony to his interest in and concern for higher education in the Midwest.

President Elliott was a great speaker because he loved our language. He treated it with personal and intellectual pride, used it like a master both in public and in private, and deeply enjoyed coining a phrase which not only emphasized the point he wished to make, but also delighted his listeners.

He could demolish a man as well as stimulate him. Certainly those who were privileged to know him or to work closely with him valued his friendship and treasured his companionship.

The life, work, and public performance of university presidents are the subject of much concern to many students of the American scene today. But what is today is always based on what happened yesterday. This book about a dynamic and remarkable university president—its facts, statements, anecdotes, and conversations—was not based solely on the author's search of the written record. It was written with the benefit of a closely personal association between the author and his subject, President Edward Charles Elliott. I therefore commend it to all who are interested in the story of higher education and those few great individuals who contributed mightily to its role in the fulfillment of the American dream.

Frederick L. Hovde
President, Purdue University

Lafayette, Indiana
March 1970

CHAPTER 1

The Early Years

Edward Charles Elliott was born in Chicago, Illinois, on December 21, 1874, the first-born of Frederick and Susan (Petts) Elliott. Frederick Elliott had been born in Ramsgate, England, on August 25, 1848; his wife, a year later on August 17. After having served as an apprentice blacksmith for seven years, he came to the United States in 1870 and worked at his trade in various cities and towns in the East and Midwest, returning to England in 1874 to marry Susan Petts on March 21 of that year. The two of them came back to Chicago within a few weeks and lived there for a little over three years. A second son, Fred, Jr., was born January 4, 1876.

In 1878 the family moved to Cedar Rapids, Iowa, where Mr. Elliott worked for the Northwestern Railroad. Two more children were born there to Frederick and Susan Elliott—a girl, Edith, and a boy, Frank. Edward started to school in Cedar Rapids in 1879 when he was four years old.

Then in 1881, the Elliotts moved to North Platte, Nebraska, where Mr. Elliott was a blacksmith and later a foreman in the Union Pacific shops. North Platte became their permanent home where the Elliotts lived (at 421 East Second Street) for more than fifty years.

The two youngest children died during the first year in North Platte, but in 1889 another son, Benjamin, was born. Fifteen years separated the eldest, Edward, from the youngest boy; but Edward and Fred, just a year apart, grew up and worked and played together with the other North Platte boys.

North Platte was a busy frontier town of perhaps fifteen hundred, largely populated with American and immigrant railroad workers and ranch hands. The Union Pacific Railroad, which had gone through only a few years earlier, was the largest source of

1

employment; North Platte was an important rail junction point and railroad repair shops were located there.

To the boys, life in North Platte consisted of chores, ballgames, make-believe Indian wars, ice skating, snow fights, school, and more chores. "My early life was the customary one of the frontier described so well by William Allen White in his autobiography," Elliott remarked.

Even though vigorously active as a boy, Edward read everything he could get his hands on. His father was an avid reader and the boy learned to get great personal satisfaction from reading. "I had a much better background in English literature when I went to the university than my children did when they finished high school," he said in later years.

Elliott's father had no advanced education but he was interested and active in local politics and was somewhat of a leader in the local labor movement. His mother spent most of her time in the home. She was a devout Episcopalian and made sure that the boys went with her to most of the Episcopal Church functions in North Platte. Edward was baptized as an Episcopalian in North Platte and attended the Episcopal Church more or less regularly throughout his life but was never confirmed.

In later years, Elliott spent little time talking about his boyhood although he liked to tell of a visit to his grandmother's home in Ramsgate. In 1887, the year of Queen Victoria's Jubilee, the family had saved enough for a summer trip to England. Edward was twelve years old, unaccustomed to travel, and taking his first ocean voyage, yet the high point of the trip for him was a day spent in London to see a former North Platte resident, "Buffalo Bill" Cody, in his Wild West Show. Cody's home was on the outskirts of North Platte and the boys had played on the river near the house many times. Just a few years before, Edward had broken through the ice while skating near there and had dried himself before the fire of the famous buffalo hunter.

Because the Elliotts were from his old home town, Cody showed them every courtesy and invited the family to dine with him in his private mess tent. Fred recalled that in the party were Cody's eldest daughter, Arta, and performers Annie Oakley and Johnny Baker. During the performance on the exposition grounds near London the Elliotts sat on front row seats and nothing about the entire vacation was more thrilling to Ed and Fred.

In 1890 young Elliott was graduated from the three-year high school in North Platte; but that year the school board voted to add a fourth year to the high school to qualify graduates to enter the university. He went back for another year (along with one other student) and was graduated from the four-year North Platte High School in 1891.

His studies in high school, he recalled, consisted of Latin, Greek, English grammar, geography, and mathematics, with textbook study (without a laboratory) in chemistry and physics. He felt that this early training in Latin and Greek accounted for his desire, amounting almost to a compulsion, for precision in both speaking and writing.

THE UNIVERSITY OF NEBRASKA

In the fall of 1891, Elliott went to Lincoln to attend the University of Nebraska where one of his selected freshman courses was chemistry. As he remembered it, the chemistry choice resulted largely from his respect and admiration for his high school chemistry instructor, M. H. Lobdell. He studied chemistry as an undergraduate major under Professor H. H. Nicholson, and was graduated with a Bachelor of Science degree in 1895.

To make money to stay in college, Elliott worked off and on at the 46 Ranch, located a few miles east of town. The 46 Ranch was owned by Charles Hendy, a friend of Elliott's father who lived in the same block and worked in the Union Pacific Shops. The Hendy boys were close friends and playmates of the Elliott boys and they, together with two or three cowboys, worked the ranch in the summer. Bill Hendy was about Edward's age, but he served as foreman when the work got under way.

The main product of the ranch was hay with cattle as a by-product. During July and August the Hendy family largely took over the work of cutting the wild hay to serve as winter feed for the cattle. The days were long and hot, the work was hard, and the pay was small, but Elliott cherished those days all of his life.

In Elliott's scrapbook of college days are stirring accounts of inter-collegiate football which he followed with intense loyalty, as well as accounts of other events which were important to him. One clipping, for example, reviewed a performance of the classical play, *Electra*, offered by the Greek and Latin departments of the university in which "Miss Willa Cather looked pleasant and happy as Electra." When I called this item to his attention, he laughed and remarked that "Willie" (who later gained national prominence as an author) was one of 66 in his class who was graduated in 1895.

In his senior year, Elliott was an active member of the committee which planned the annual "Senior Promenade" and a few days later appeared in the Senior Class Day skit which "provoked much laughter."

Also in his final year he worked especially hard with the cadets in Company C of a cadet batallion. The Cadet Corps under Lt. John J. Pershing, who served as military instructor at the University from 1891 to 1895, was rigorously trained for the annual drill contest for the possession of the Omaha Cup. When the competitive drills were held in May 1895, Company C placed second and Lt. Pershing presented Elliott with the sword that had been used to drill the company during the year. It remained one of his prized possessions for fifty years until he presented it to Purdue University a few weeks after he had retired as president in 1945.

Elliott kept in occasional contact with Pershing during the years that followed his graduation and when Pershing retired in 1924, Elliott wrote to the General saying that he would always treasure the memory of Pershing "as a great teacher as well as a great leader." Elliott noted that Pershing's farewell message and President Coolidge's message of appreciation had caused him to be "more keenly aware than ever before of the great obligation which all of us have who were privileged to spend those four, unforgetable years with you at the University of Nebraska."

Pershing promptly wrote in reply, "Please permit me to say that your friendship and support have always been an inspiration to me, and to extend to you my warmest congratulations on your own services to our country."

Six years later Elliott visited with Pershing in his Washington office on the occasion of Pershing's 70th birthday. His admiration for Pershing continued for as long as he lived, and many times he commented that his own erect posture was a result of the training he had received under Pershing. When his own children slouched at the dinner table, he more than once said, "Sit up straight and get those shoulders back or I'll have to get a brace for you."

He was a strong proponent of physical fitness programs and took his simple "setting-up exercises" every morning, he said, largely because Pershing had once said to him, "Young man, you have a good body. Take care of it." The fact that he was an advocate of universal military training, as is detailed later, was surely almost entirely a result of Pershing's influence.

Elliott recalled that there were several outstanding men at the university during those years whose friendship meant a great deal to him. Along with Nicholson in the Chemistry Department was John White, who later was head of the Department of Chemistry at Rose Polytechnic for 34 years, and George B. Frankforter, later dean of the School of Chemistry at the University of Minnesota. During his senior year Elliott was an errand boy and messenger for Chancellor James A. Canfield, who afterwards served as president of Ohio State University and whose daughter, Dorothy Canfield Fisher, was a favorite of Elliott's.

Elliott had hoped to get a teaching position in a high school following graduation in 1895. He made applications at several schools but for various reasons did not sign a contract. At graduation he accepted a teaching assistantship with Nicholson for two more years. In June 1897, he was graduated with the degree of Master of Arts. Edward Everett Hale addressed the graduates.

Still hoping to teach, Elliott was looking forward to further study in Germany following the approved pattern of the times, but money was scarce. These were hard times in Nebraska and Elliott had no choice but to find a job.

Professor Nicholson assisted him in the search for a teaching position noting that Elliott was "a young man of most sterling worth and ability." In his letter of recommendation he said that Elliott had "natural teaching ability of a high order; takes an interest in his work and in his pupils and, not only does he secure the best results from them, but also keeps a genuine respect."

While investigating various job prospects during the spring of 1897, Elliott learned that there was a position open in the new high school at Omaha. He took the required examination in physics, chemistry, and mathematics, passed with distinction and was being favorably considered for the position by Superintendent C. G. Pearse when a Dr. Senter, an older man just returned from Germany with a Ph.D. degree, made application and got the job. It was a bitter disappointment.

Superintendent Pearse, who had made the decision not to hire Elliott, later went to Milwaukee, Wisconsin, as superintendent of schools and became president of Wisconsin State Normal School. Elliott enjoyed telling me that during his years in Wisconsin he and Pearse appeared together on many programs. Elliott, then a professor of education at Wisconsin, chided Pearse on several occasions about his failure to give him the job in Omaha. Pearse retaliated, with a smile on his face, by telling audiences that

Professor Elliott owed him money, since Pearse had forced him to move on. "If it hadn't been for me," concluded Pearse, "Professor Elliott might still be in Omaha, teaching science for the next forty years."

Later in the spring of 1897, Elliott happened to chat with Professor C. E. Bessey of the Botany Department. As Elliott recalled it, Bessey suggested that he apply for a teaching position in the Leadville, Colorado, high school. Acting on Bessey's recommendation, Elliott got the job and went to Leadville to teach science during the 1897-1898 school term.

LEADVILLE, COLORADO

Leadville, known all over the country in the late 1800's as a prosperous mining town, had suffered economically by reason of the demonetization of silver in 1893. Whereas in the '80s it had been a wild booming mining town of about 10,000 inhabitants, a disastrous strike had diminished prosperity and the population had declined in the years immediately following the government decree. Gone were most of the tents and temporary dwellings as were most of the gambling "hells" and saloons which had crowded the business section.

By 1897, however, a pronounced revival could readily be seen. As mining operations stablized, the population began to grow again and the citizens evidenced a new interest in civic undertakings. Elliott recalled that the more stable elements of the population seemed to be gradually gaining control. Schools were important to people who planned to establish permanent homes for their children. In many respects it was a favorable time for a young man to accept a position in the schools.

Nevertheless this rough frontier mining town must have looked bleak and forbidding as Elliott arrived on August 30, 1897, during a driving snowstorm, riding in an open freight car with $5.00 in his pocket! The new teacher had been forced to transfer to the open freight car because a train wreck had torn up the track a few miles out of town.

Elliott obtained a single room in a private home and took his meals at a boarding house around the corner, patronized almost entirely by miners. He was twenty-two years old and "as green as they come," he said.

He found that his laboratory equipment consisted of twelve bunsen burners in various states of repair. During that first year

Elliott worked diligently to build equipment so that his courses in physics and chemistry might include more than the minimum of laboratory experiments. He spent much of his free time fashioning crude but workable laboratory fixtures.

Elliott had little to say about that first year in Leadville except for three incidents, all of which happened during a single week in the spring of 1898.

In May 1898, he was invited to attend a party given by one of the socially prominent and brilliant ladies of Leadville, Miss Elizabeth Nowland, daughter of school board member and local publisher John Nowland. Elliott considered himself to be one of the "extra" young men in town and was happy to be able to attend the little party since he seldom was included in the local group this first year.

He never forgot the night; but only partly because Elizabeth Nowland later became Mrs. Elliott. On that particular Friday evening Elliott had stayed after school to help a student complete an experiment in photometrics. The darkroom consisted of a classroom corner enclosed in black draperies equipped with candles in hand-made bases, all constructed by the first-year teacher. Elliott left the student still working at 4 p.m. in order to get ready for the evening party.

At breakfast the next morning the boarding house talk was all about the bad fire at the schoolhouse the night before. Too excited to eat breakfast, Elliott ran over to the school to learn that the temporary darkroom had gone up in flames and a considerable amount of damage had been done to that section of the building before the flames were extinguished. Elliott was uneasy to say the least. He awaited the expected summons of the school board but it was not until the following Thursday that he was called to meet with the board members. The week had passed with agonizing slowness.

As he greeted the board, however, he could discern no antagonism, and after the amenities, the president of the board, Charles Cavender, announced that they had selected Elliott to serve as superintendent of schools for the following year with the generous salary of $1,500 per year. The fire was not even mentioned, and Superintendent Elliott left with his head in the clouds.

While there is little on record to establish the caliber of his teaching, there was evidence that the board members thought well of his work in the school. Within a few weeks, Elliott recalled, he was offered a job as a chemist at an Idaho agricultural experiment station. Even though his training indicated that he was probably better qualified in chemistry, the higher salary offered at Leadville sold him on the job as superintendent of schools. During the summer he went back to the University of Nebraska to take some courses in education and followed this with some correspondence work under psychology professor Arthur Allin at the University of Colorado. During the next several years he continued his part-time study of education.

THE NEW SUPERINTENDENT

The Leadville school system, which included the high school and five elementary schools enrolling more than 1,500 pupils, was faced with organization, enrollment, and curricular problems which required constant study from an expert administrator. Elliott began his work with enthusiasm and immediately set about codifying the various rules and regulations which heretofore had not been recorded.

By June 1899, he had formulated a set of regulations governing the certification and appointment of teachers, followed by regulations governing the salaries and contracts of teachers. For the first time a salary schedule was established and the professional and scholastic qualifications of Leadville teachers were fixed by a definite system.

By July, a list of by-laws and rules and regulations had been meticulously prepared listing general rules and rules governing the duties of the superintendent, principals, teachers, pupils, and janitors.

The following July, Elliott sent the school board exhaustive outlines of the courses of study for the primary grammar schools and high school of the district. They were adopted by August.

This was routine administrative work; but the annual reports to the school board provide a rather complete account of the thoroughness with which he undertook to serve the mining community and present a remarkably clear picture of the principles and ideals which he developed during this formative period at Leadville.

Among other things, he was concerned with attendance and directed attention to the inadequacy of the compulsory attendance laws, but he was even more disturbed over the lack of proper accommodations. By 1903, he was insisting that many of the buildings either be reconditioned or torn down and replaced. Some of the buildings were totally unfit for school purposes, he said, and various rooms in other buildings lacked suitable lighting and ventilation. Exasperated by the lack of sanitation, he once wrote "the present plan of providing drinking water to the pupils of the elementary schools is a relic of the days of school administration when the word *sanitation* was unknown."

He pointed out that the facilities for providing drinking water consisted of two or three water pails, to which were attached by chains a half dozen or more tin cups. In some cases several hundred pupils were drinking water from these pails, providing in his words, "prolific sources of contagion among the school children."

Leadville was no model of municipal cleanliness and neatness, he observed, but "if there is one institution in the community that should stand for cleanliness and the observance of those conditions of recognized hygienic and sanitary value, that institution is the public school." He insisted that "the school cannot preach, cannot teach, cleanliness and that regard for personal hygiene as long as its practices are as they are."

In December 1898, Elliott visited the state university in an attempt to have the three-year high school placed on the university's accredited list. Professor Allin made a personal inspection of the Leadville High School, but refused to recognize the work of the school as equivalent to the university requirements for admission.

Elliott immediately renewed his earlier recommendation to the board that the high school course be lengthened to four years and the board responded with a favorable vote. Before the end of his first year in office, the taxpayers had voted to contract a bonded indebtedness of $45,000 for the purpose of purchasing a site, building and furnishing a high school building. The high school opened in September 1899 as a four-year high school with an elective system, and the new building was occupied in the spring of 1900.

During the first year the eighth grade was taught by high school instructors in the same building, but there were problems with this arrangement. So in May 1900, the eighth grade was incorporated as an integral part of the high school and the new high school course was for five years, the seventh grade marking the end of the elementary school course.

The new graduated salary schedule had raised the minimum salary to a living point and had done away with constant demands from the teachers for salary increases. Nevertheless, Elliott expressed concern over the fact that teachers were being paid less than the common laborer in the community. One of his final appeals to the board was for higher teacher salaries. Pointing out that each year 25 to 30 percent of the Leadville teaching staff were new teachers, he said, "Is it to be marveled at that our high school teachers are continually leaving for better posi- tions, when $1,000 is the limitation placed on their services?"

Elliott wanted good teachers and he was convinced that sal- aries had to be raised before he could expect to get the successful teachers that were needed.

The schedule of teachers' meetings which Elliott directed was a rather heavy one in the light of present-day practices. During the school year 1898-1899 the entire faculty studied James' psy- chology while the following year was devoted to the study of gen- eral teaching methods. Later yearly schedules consisted of special meetings at which papers were read by different teachers who had specialized knowledge or prominent school men of the state were invited in to deliver lectures on special topies. As a general rule these meetings were held at least twice, and sometimes three times, a month.

At the same time he was working to improve the faculty, how- ever, he also made attempts to enlist the parents' support of the work of the schools. In the fall of 1901 he sent a letter to parents asking their cooperation, pointing out that irregular attendance did not help the work in school. He also asked that parents dis- courage their children from attending social gatherings scheduled during the week nights because, "these diversions usually bring about a waste of energy and vitality needed for a proper prep- aration of school tasks."

The letter raised no great amount of adverse criticism or comment from the school patrons apparently, although some par- ents were aroused to reply that these things were "none of his business," Elliott recalled.

Even as he worked to build a better school system for Lead- ville, Elliott was also concerned with the office of the superin- tendent and the requirements of the position.

Speaking before the students at the Colorado State Normal School in Greeley on "The Relation of the Superintendent and the Teacher," he noted that the fundamental duty of the superin- tendent was "to supervise, to direct methods of instruction, and to establish the standards of instruction." The superintendent, he thought, should be "the educational expert, upon whom the progress of our schools and the solution of their problems is to devolve."

Elliott had had little opportunity to make a study of the administrative responsibilities involved in the superintendency, yet he was perhaps as well prepared for the position as any young man whom the board might have selected. At the turn of the century school administrative procedures had been the object of very little careful scientific study.

As it later developed, his decision to work as an administrator was a timely one, for the next few decades saw the development of an extensive movement to professionalize school administration. While Elliott's views on educational matters at this early date were not always of consequence, they had some significance in that they indicated his immediate acceptance of parts of an educational philosophy which later gained widespread approval.

His repeated pleas for higher salaries for example, were in line with well-established policies. As early as 1835 the need for higher salaries for teachers had been emphasized, and the relationship between low salaries and incompetent personnel had been pointed out again and again. However, the fact that Elliott advocated some kind of a salary *schedule,* based on training and experience, is of more than a little interest. The establishment of definite salary schedules was largely a development of the twentieth century, and only since World War I has there been a rapid trend toward schedules based on training and experience.[1]

Elliott further developed the idea of the superintendent as an educational expert and supervisor while he was at the University of Wisconsin.

TEACHERS COLLEGE

The thought of further education frequently recurred to Elliott during his six years at Leadville. The idea of professional schools of education was gaining nationwide recognition and one of the most prominent of these developing schools was Teachers College, which had been reorganized at Columbia University in 1898.

Professor James E. Russell, a colleague of Allin at the University of Colorado, had moved to Columbia University in 1897, and the following year was made dean of the newly-reorganized Teachers College. He, together with Professor E. L. Thorndike and Professor Paul Monroe, set out to recruit top young men in education for the new graduate school.

Russell learned of Elliott through the strong recommendation of Allin, and, during the summer of 1899 at a National Education Association Department of Superintendence meeting, Russell met Elliott and talked to him about coming to Teachers College. At that time Elliott felt that his financial situation would not permit his leaving Leadville.

Then in 1901, Professor John Dewey, who was attempting to build a strong graduate program in education at the University of Chicago, offered him a fellowship to start there in September; still Elliott could not afford to accept any offer.

But early in 1903 at an N. E. A. meeting in Cincinnati, Elliott was again interviewed by Professors Russell, Thorndike, and Monroe. They offered him a fellowship at Teachers College which he accepted within a few weeks after he had returned to Leadville.

Professor Allin's persistent urging had finally succeeded. He had been in frequent contact with Elliott because it was his job to inspect the public schools of the state for the university, and he had been encouraging Elliott to get further training. He was of the opinion that the Leadville schools, under Elliott's leadership, had made greater progress than had any other school system in the state. Impressed with Elliott's "clear foresight, able management, and scholarship," he considered Elliott "a first-class man and a first-class superintendent."

So Elliott spent the school year of 1903-1904 as an assistant in education administration at Columbia. The following summer he went to the University of Jena, Germany, (in part, at least, to prepare for the language requirement emphasized at Teachers College). There he observed work in the German schools and attended lectures by Professor William Rein. Later in the summer he traveled in Germany, Switzerland, France, spending part of the time with classmates Walter F. Dearborn and Ellwood P. Cubberley.

He closed out his trip by going to England to visit with relatives in London and Ramsgate. He could remember only a few of the things that he had seen there in 1887, he reported to his father, but uncles and aunts and cousins fed him "beefsteak pudding and apple dumplings" until he could eat no more. They talked with him for hours about his parents, their visit 17 years earlier, and life in the United States.

When he returned in the fall (sporting a handsome beard that he had grown during the summer) he began his second year at Teachers College as a teaching fellow. "That second year, when

I began teaching courses in administration for Professor S. T. Dutton, was when I made my final decision to work in educational administration," Elliott later recalled.

Elliott's work at Teachers College at this particular time has a special significance for students of education. With considerable effort the faculty at Teachers College had gathered a select group of promising students. Along with Elliott were Cubberley, who later served as a dean of the School of Education at Stanford from 1917-1933; Henry Suzzalo, who became president of the University of Washington and later president of the Carnegie Foundation for the Advancement of Teaching; George D. Strayer, who stayed on at Columbia as a professor of education for 38 years; Dearborn, who spent nearly forty years in the graduate school of education at Harvard; Bruce R. Payne, who served as president of the George Peabody College for Teachers from 1911-1937; and Junius L. Meriam, professor of education at the University of California at Los Angeles from 1924-1943.

These men all received their degrees in 1905. The famous series of Teachers College *Contributions to Education* began with this group. Meriam began the series with Number 1; Cubberley wrote Number 2; Suzzalo, 3; J. A. MacVannel, 4; Strayer, 5; and Elliott, 6.

Elliott's contribution was his doctoral dissertation, *Some Fiscal Aspects of Public Education in American Cities*. Much of this work was done under the direction of Thorndike, an acknowledged early leader in educational psychology, who was the first to apply the latest scientific techniques and methods to education.

Twenty years later Cubberley wrote that the early work in the application of statistical procedures to the study of educational problems began in 1902-1903. "The first fruits of this method, as applied to school administration, came in 1905," he wrote, "with the publication of two Teachers College doctor's dissertations, one by Elliott . . . and the other by Strayer . . . ."

Elliott recalled that while working on his dissertation, however, he had some disagreements with Thorndike and finally went to see President Nicholas Murray Butler to talk over the matter. Butler was a good listener and by the time the conversation was over, he had charmed Elliott completely; the problems with Thorndike no longer seemed to be major ones. It was the beginning of a life-long friendship, and Elliott thought that it may have led to his going to the University of Wisconsin.

Elliott happened to be in Butler's office in the spring of 1905 when Dean E. A. Birge and President Charles R. Van Hise of the

University of Wisconsin stopped in to see Butler about employing Teachers College graduates for positions at their university.

Van Hise and Birge were specifically looking to Teachers College to supply outstanding men for the work of training teachers for the rapidly growing public school system in the state. Butler gave an on-the-spot personal recommendation for Elliott which, of course, was later substantiated by the personal and professional recommendations of Russell, Thorndike, and Monroe.

Thus in the fall of 1905, Elliott reported to Madison as an associate professor in education, along with classmate Walter Dearborn, a newly appointed instructor in educational psychology.

NOTES

1. R. F. Butts and L. A. Cremin, *A History of Education in American Culture* (New York: Henry Holt and Company, 1953), pp. 232, 399, 602.

CHAPTER 2

The University of Wisconsin

"I had very little money when I arrived in Madison," Elliott said, "and was happy when Walter Dearborn and his wife offered to rent a room in their home to me. I guess he needed money, too." So Elliott moved in and remained with the Dearborns for two years.

His job at the university consisted primarily of teaching assignments in the College of Letters and Science, but within a year Elliott was named chairman of the Committee on Accrediting of High Schools, a post which during the next few years caused him to be in frequent contact with President Van Hise and State Superintendent of Public Instruction, Charles P. Cary. Van Hise and Cary were incompatible and it eventually fell to Elliott to act as a liaison person between the two. He found himself immediately in the midst of complicated relationships between the university and the State Department of Public Instruction. That story is detailed later, but there is every evidence that Elliott performed his assigned tasks well.

At the end of two years Elliott was promoted to professor of education, his salary was increased from $2,000 to $2,500, and he moved to establish his own home with his bride, Elizabeth Nowland Elliott.

A warm friendship had developed between the two young people during Elliott's years in Leadville, and when he left in 1903 for New York, they had agreed to continue their friendship by correspondence. The Nowlands were moving at the same time from Leadville to a small farm near Spokane, Washington, because of Mr. Nowland's poor health.

Elliott did not see Miss Nowland for the next three years although they wrote regularly and apparently with increasing fervor; for in the early spring of 1906, Elliott traveled to California by way of Spokane. Ostensibly the trip was made to confer with friend Ellwood Cubberley at Stanford about a series of books on education which the two proposed to write. The more lasting agreement was made in Spokane, however, for while Cubberley and Elliott worked closely together for the next ten years, Elliott and Miss Nowland made an agreement which lasted a lifetime. They made plans to be married.

Elliott's visit to the West Coast was a brief one since he had agreed to work that summer in Washington, D. C., with Commissioner Elmer Ellsworth Brown on the first of a series of legislative summaries which he prepared for the Federal Bureau of Education. It was a hectic summer for the newly-engaged couple; as Elliott remarked later, "We fixed things up between us in the spring, and the rest of the summer I vibrated between Washington, D. C., and Spokane."

The following spring (1907) Elliott (who had just received his promotion) and Elizabeth Nowland were married in Spokane, Washington, on June 15.

Because Elliott had agreed to teach a course in educational administration at Teachers College during the summer of 1907, their honeymoon was a trip from Spokane to New York City.

On the way East, Elliott and his bride stopped at the University of Illinois at the request of President Edmund James. James, who was avowedly out to beat Wisconsin by setting up a stronger Department of Education, offered Elliott a job in the department; but Elliott was excited with the prospect in Madison and not at all anxious to leave his work there. Elliott recalled that the day which the young couple spent in Champaign was "a scorcher," and although the bride had never been in Madison, she was sure that she didn't want to live in Illinois.

This was merely the first of many offers which came to Elliott during the next ten years because as universities over the country started developing departments of education, the leaders in the field were very much in demand. Cubberley frequently asked Elliott to join him at Stanford, and Charles H. Judd, another close friend for many years, wanted him at the University of Chicago. Judd, succeeding John Dewey as dean of the School of Education, had hoped to get Cubberley, Suzzalo, and Elliott among others to set up what he thought would be the strongest program in the nation, but none of the three wanted to leave his own work.

Judd nearly succeeded in 1909 when he and Harry Pratt Judson, president of the University of Chicago, offered Elliott an increase of $1,000 to come there. Elliott was about to accept but Van Hise and Birge countered by naming him director of the Course for the Training of Teachers at the same salary he would have gotten at Chicago ($3,500) so he stayed in Madison—but it was close. Elliott did teach at the University of Chicago summer session in 1911, however.

After a summer in New York, the Elliotts established their first home in Madison, where all four of the Elliott's children were born. The first boy, John, was born April 24, 1908; Susanne, December 22, 1910; Marion, December 4, 1912; and Edward, January 11, 1915.

It was not until 1910 that the Elliotts built their own home at 137 Prospect Avenue in Madison, the only home they ever owned. They expected to stay in Madison and had come to an agreement that they would not leave merely to work at another university.

They started a garden in the back yard where they raised a variety of vegetables and had a berry patch which included gooseberries, currants, and raspberries—the latter probably Elliott's favorite fruit. John remembered that his dad was especially proud of his asparagus bed and their tomatoes. And although John liked the abundance of gooseberry jam that his mother made, it took him years to learn to like carrots and turnips because they had so many when he was a small boy. Even well into the winter his dad seemed to have a limitless supply stored in the basement in boxes filled with sand.

In 1912 Elliott's younger brother, Ben, accepted a fellowship and came to the University of Wisconsin for advanced study. He lived just down the street from his older brother and, after receiving his degree in 1913, stayed on for another year as an instructor. All of the Elliotts loved Madison and Ben later returned to the campus and had a distinguished career as professor of mechanical engineering at the university.

During the ten and one half years Elliott spent at Madison, his tremendous output of scholarly work was amazingly varied, and much of it remains as a testimonial to his apparently boundless energy. Partly as a result of his scholarly activities and partly because of his skill in handling the problems associated with the Van Hise-Cary relationship, attention was directed to his administrative skill and vigor, and he became widely recognized as a leader in the field of school administration. Thus, when the Board of Regents in 1908 established a new plan for teacher training at the university, the Course for the Training of Teachers, Elliott was named director of the new administrative unit, a post which he held from 1909 to 1916, the year he left the university to go to the University of Montana.

Because Elliott was active in many areas of concern to educators during his stay at the University of Wisconsin, it is difficult to organize his work into a chronological order. His first activities in addition to teaching, however, related to the problem of accreditation of high schools, as was mentioned earlier, and from this beginning he moved into other areas of work.

THE PROBLEM OF ACCREDITATION

The University of Wisconsin had assumed the responsibility of inspecting and accrediting high schools throughout the state several years before Elliott joined the staff. It was the accepted practice to admit to the university only those pupils who had graduated from an accredited high school. Unfortunately, there was considerable disagreement as to who should do the inspecting and accrediting. A "war" developed between State Superintendent Charles P. Cary and the university which lasted from 1902 to 1921, the entire time Cary was in office.

At first Cary attacked only the system of inspection and accreditation of public schools by the university, but he later expanded his complaints to include teaching and political activity of university people. Protesting, he pointed out that the high schools had many functions other than preparing students for college, and that the university must give up its inspection and accept graduates of all high schools.

As the man named to work with Cary, Elliott was in a precarious position. He found himself attempting to set up a strong department of education, a department which Dean Birge and Superintendent Cary favored; but he was doing this against considerable opposition from the academic departments, an opposition tolerated by Van Hise. At the same time he was in charge of the university Committee on Accrediting, strongly favored by President Van Hise and bitterly opposed by Superintendent Cary.

The problems were never completely solved during Elliott's years at Madison, but he remained friendly with Cary and progress was made as a result of his attempts to establish a closer working relationship between the university and the public school system.

As he worked to build a teacher training program which would be integrated with the public school system, Elliott refrained from

speaking or writing articles which might fan the flames of contention. The annual reports of the Committee on Accredited Schools
(with Elliott as chairman) carefully avoided the strife between the
state department and the university, for example.

Elliott, however, was responsible for two studies which were
directly connected with the problem of accrediting high schools;
the first was started in 1909 by Dearborn and Elliott to show the
relative standings of pupils in the high school and the university.
But Elliott soon withdrew from the project because his rather
close working relationship with Cary made it awkward for him
to complete the study. When the paper was published (by Dearborn) it concluded that the academic ranking of pupils in high
school furnished a satisfactory means for predicting the likelihood
of successful work at a university. Elliott's written introduction to
Dearborn's study observed that "only a specious skepticism would
deny that there was no correlation between secondary school success and college success."

At about the same time, Elliott had begun working on a second study to establish the degree of reliability or unreliability of
the grading of high school work. Since the preliminary findings
emphasized the differences existing between high schools of the
state, Dean Birge advised him to hold off on this study for a few
years in view of the strained relations between the university
and the State Department of Education. While Cary was saying
in essence that all secondary schools were alike, this study proved
that tremendous inequalities existed.

THE RELIABILITY OF GRADING IN HIGH SCHOOL

Elliott had gone far enough in his investigation to prove to
himself that the grading of high school papers was characterized
by an astonishingly wide range of variation. During the next few
years his interest in the problem was shared by psychologist Daniel
Starch who had come to the university as an instructor in 1907.
Starch was eight years younger than Elliott but he was a good
friend and eager to work on the investigation. Starch worked out
the statistical details of the study, and in 1912, an account of
their first work was published in *School Review* listing Starch and
Elliott as the co-authors.

The method of study which they devised is familiar to many
students of education. Two identical papers were graded by 142
English teachers located throughout the state. The general results
indicated that there was a wide range of variation, that beginning

teachers without experience marked more generously than teachers with experience, and that teachers in small high schools tended to mark somewhat higher than teachers in large high schools.

As soon as these results appeared, the cry was raised that even though there was considerable variation in English, the more exact courses, such as mathematics, would show a different pattern.

Accepting the challenge, the same authors published a second article six months later in the same magazine which described a similar study, this time in mathematics.

In their second study, a set of questions and a copy of the answer paper were sent to approximately 180 high schools in the North Central Association with the request that the principal teacher in mathematics grade this paper according to the practices and standards of the school. The investigation showed an extremely wide variation of the grades even more forcibly than had their study of English papers.

Eight months later the two published a third article, this time reporting on a study using examination papers in history. The study followed virtually the same procedure used in the two proceeding studies and the results were much the same. The authors concluded that the variability or unreliability of grades is as great in one subject as in another for the findings with the history paper fully corroborated the findings with the English and mathematics papers.

The authors suggested that all schools should come up with some uniform marking system so that the variability could be reduced. They concluded that courses in education should give instruction regarding the technique and methods of marking and evaluating school work so that teachers in training would appreciate the problems involved in grading.

Elliott wrote no other articles in this particular area of study, but Starch published at least one additional study. References to these significant studies are to be found in practically all standard volumes on educational psychology or educational measurements; and Remmers and Gage reported in 1943 that Starch and Elliott were the first to demonstrate the unreliability of grading essay tests.[1]

THE TRAINING OF TEACHERS

The primary duties assigned to Elliott, regardless of the extra work involved in attempting to maintain a working relationship with the State Department of Instruction, were centered on establishing a strong teacher training program in the department of education. His other activities were always secondary to his main responsibility as director of the Course for the Training of Teachers.

Teacher training had held Elliott's interest even at Leadville, and this interest continued while he was at Teachers College. As early as 1905, Elliott had written a paper for the National Society for the Scientific Study of Education in which he paid particular attention to teacher qualifications and the early laws regarding teacher training and certification.

After working for four years in a loosely organized department at Wisconsin, Elliott welcomed a program which gave some semblance of order to the task of training teachers. He believed wholeheartedly in the work of the secondary school, he recognized the important place of the teacher in the school, and he thought he knew the characteristics of a good teacher. Here was his opportunity to direct a program to train teachers.

In Elliott's view one of the more important initial steps taken in his first years as director was the completion of a formal agreement between the Board of Regents of the University and the Board of Education of the city of Madison.

The first agreement called for a maximum of five teachers to be appointed jointly by the city schools and the university to serve in the Madison High School. These instructors were to teach not more than fifteen hours per week and their classes were to be open for special visitation and observational study by university students. The university agreed to pay two-thirds and the board of education one-third of the annual salary of each of these teachers. In addition, certain regularly employed high school teachers were selected to receive $10.00 per month for each month during which time their classes were to be open for visitation and observation.

Elliott felt that in the absence of an organized secondary school under the complete control and direction of the university, this cooperative plan with the Madison High School provided at least a minimum of laboratory experience for the student teacher.

Within a few months a second agreement was made which included some of the elementary schools in order that those elementary teachers who were in training could also receive the benefits of supervised teacher training in the Madison public schools.

Even with these facilities, however, Elliott felt that the Course for the Training of Teachers would be severely handicapped until such time as a secondary school to be used as a laboratory for those students in training could be established under the complete control of the university.

In 1910 Elliott proposed that each public school teacher be required to complete a five-year training program before receiving an unlimited certificate. He felt that four years of training should qualify a student for a limited certificate but that a First Grade Secondary School Certificate should not be awarded until five years of training had been completed.

The legal requirement for licensing at this time, however, called only for four years training in order to receive an unlimited teachers license. Without legal sanction there was little incentive for the fifth year of training and Elliott eventually concluded that ". . . four years is the limit that the American secondary education traffic will bear . . . ." Today, of course, many of the states (including Indiana) issue a provisional teaching certificate after four years training and grant an unlimited certificate only after five years of training. Elliott's proposal came 40 years too soon!

Later Elliott wrote that teaching required a preparation as carefully devised and as intensive as that required "for the lawyer, the doctor, the engineer, or the agriculturalist." "The state and its schools need not only better teachers but more teachers, and above all more men teachers," he continued. He felt that teachers were entitled to more social respect and to larger salaries and he urged the alumni of the university to become more interested in the teachers working in the public schools.

Elliott continued to plead for the establishment of a university-controlled secondary school to serve for observation and practice and for the training of teachers. President Van Hise carried this request to the legislature and, finally, funds were appropriated for this purpose.

Thus the Wisconsin High School was established largely as a result of Elliott's persistent efforts. The school opened in 1911 in rented quarters but it was not until September, 1914, that the Wisconsin High School building was completed and occupied. According to Elliott, Wisconsin was the second large state university "to enter definitely upon the project of a school of this type."

The idea of providing teacher training through a university department of education had had its development in the 1870's and by 1900 nearly 250 universities had established departments or chairs of education. The practice of having a special secondary school under the control of the university for the purpose of observation and supervision of the student teachers, however, was a relatively new practice in 1911.

The high school had its critics, however, and one of the most active was W. H. Allen, an educator who had been employed by the Wisconsin State Board of Affairs in 1914 to conduct a survey of the University of Wisconsin.[2] The reasons for the survey were highly complex and only incidentally related to the teacher training program but it turned out that one of the prime targets of the Allen survey was the Wisconsin High School. "Why Mr. Allen should have attacked this school at Madison with such vigor, not to say virilence," wrote Professor George H. Mead of the University of Chicago in 1915, "is quite incomprehensible from the report." Allen attacked the building, its equipment, its forms of registration, and opposed the expenditure of state money for its purpose.[3]

Elliott responded with seventy-five pages of comments defending his position and concluded that "In respect to the study of the very important problem of the training of teachers, Mr. Allen has failed with a characteristic completeness to utilize a large opportunity to render a real service."

Other leaders in education (and friends of Elliott) joined the chorus of protests, but Cubberley at Stanford was particularly vehement. He later wrote that "the so-called survey of the University of Wisconsin was a most outrageous investigation. One cannot read the report," he continued, "without feeling that the activating purpose of those in charge of the survey was criticism and agitation."

After half a dozen years as director of the Course for the Training of Teachers, Elliott summarized his thoughts on teacher training before a meeting of the Wisconsin Teachers Association in November 1914. He suggested that none of the teacher training institutions had found the best way to educate and train teachers for service in the schools, and no teacher training institution could prepare students for immediate, competent service upon graduation. "The greatest immediate need for the effective training of our teachers," he said, "is the existence of a body of skilled principals and supervisors who know how to capitalize into service . . . those recent graduates of training institutions." He also suggested that each teacher training institution needed to provide a better organized and more constructive plan for "following up, assisting, and guiding our young teachers during their first year of service."

After ten years in the work of training teachers, Elliott could look back on an extensive list of accomplishments. Many of his original ideas had been more completely developed, some ideas discarded, and occasional new plans devised to fit the ever-expanding work. The early enthusiasm had been tempered by experience, but the basic drive to reform, to improve public education was still present.

In their history of the University of Wisconsin, Curti and Carstensen favorably reviewed the work done by Elliott and the committee in setting up the arrangements with the Madison public schools and the later development, the Wisconsin High School.[4] Regarding the efforts to increase the amount of special training for teachers, however, they noted that when the faculty increased the requirements for the University Teachers Certificate from twelve semester hours to seventeen semester hours in 1914, they had exceeded the strict requirements of the state department and a few years later the university's attempts to establish higher standards for teachers had to be rescinded. Few prospective teachers were willing to take the additional course work and, after Elliott left the university, the faculty voted to reduce the amount of professional work for a teacher's certificate to fifteen hours and the fifth year course for teachers was dropped.

Elliott spent the better part of a decade struggling to build an outstanding department of education, but it became clear that he was fighting a losing battle to raise teacher's standards to a point which he considered necessary. By 1915, Elliott was in a proper state of mind to consider changing positions. It was not that he had suffered a complete defeat, but the prospect of leading a department which promised to deteriorate into an ordinary teacher training course was no challenge when compared to the offer to go to Montana as chancellor, a post which had just been created. This offer, of course, came late in 1915, and it would be an injustice to move on without regard for the countless other activities which marked his career at Wisconsin.

MEASURING TEACHER MERIT

One of the more interesting by-products of his work to train more and better teachers for the high schools was his scheme for measuring teacher efficiency. In 1910 Elliott developed a rating scale for teachers which he published as his *Provisional Plan For The Measure of Merit of Teachers.* He liked to say that he got the idea for his rating scale, a sort of score card for teachers, from a neighboring professor who was using a similar rating scale to judge poultry contests.

The first public description of the rating scale was made before the State Convention of City Superintendents in Madison as a result of Superintendent Cary's invitation to speak. Elliott worked intermittently with the rating scale during the next three or four years and finally had it copyrighted in 1914.

In 1914 and 1915, Elliott talked about his rating scale before the National Education Association, the South Dakota Teachers Association and at least six other groups. In the meantime his description of the plan was published in *Educational Administration and Supervision, The Toledo Teacher,* and *The Educational Monthly.*

Of course, when Elliott went to Montana the following year, he had to give up these activities and drop any future plans he may have had for perfecting the device.

Apparently the rating scale worked out by Elliott was the first device of this type to be published. In 1950, Domas and Tiedeman published an exhaustive study listing 1,006 articles on measuring teacher competency that had been published from 1894 to 1949.[5] The eighteen articles published prior to 1910 simply listed the qualifications or characteristics of a good teacher, discussed the validity of estimates of merit made by principals or supervisors without the use of a rating scale, or described estimates of merit made by pupils.

In reviewing the work of measuring the merit of teachers, Professor Jesse B. Sears at Stanford in 1921 wrote, "the writer has found no study that bears at all directly upon the subject that was made before 1905, and no carefully devised rating scheme appeared before that of Elliott's. . . ." It appears that Elliott had opened a new field of investigation.[6]

The entire problem of rating teachers has been a major topic for discussion since the beginning of the century. Plans have been advanced for the rating of teachers by pupils, supervisors, college grades, aptitude tests, and pupil growth. The question of what qualities should be measured ranged from lengthy, detailed lists including the culture and refinement of the teacher to abbreviated lists of perhaps three traits. Many of the recent articles point to salary schedules based on merit ratings, while others demand that rating scales should be used only to help teachers become more efficient. Still others insist that rating scales are worthless unless based on pupil progress alone.

Elliott made his position clear on most of these issues in 1915. In a talk before the N. E. A. Department of Superintendence he justified the use of a rating scale by saying, "experience and observation bulwarks my contention that the teacher is an octo-personality (sic); that there is a physical teacher, a moral teacher, an executive teacher, a supervisory teacher, and finally an achievement teacher . . . ." He went on to say, however, that any measure of teachers' efficiency "must reward variety of ideas instead of uniformity of ideas, flexibility of procedure rather than rigidity, the plan of individuality in place of readiness of adaptation to the machine."

THE RURAL SCHOOL

One of the early additional assignments which fell to Elliott was the specific study of rural schools. The university on several occasions sent him to Ohio and Indiana to study consolidation, transportation, and other problems confronting schools in rural areas.

At the same time he and Cubberley were working together, writing about the problems of rural school administration. The first indication of this interest occurred in the spring of 1907 when his article in the *Educational Review* praised the County School Board Convention as a notable movement to raise the standards and increase the efficiency of the American rural school. This essay was only a brief notice of his interest, but the next several years saw him take an active part in the wider movement to improve rural school conditions.

In 1909, he prepared a series of four articles for the *Atlantic Educational Journal* in which he presented certain aspects of rural education which seemed to him to be "large and important factors in determining the success of the rural school as an instrument for the general uplift of social conditions as these exist outside of cities."

He began this series by describing a group of difficulties confronting the rural students. The first, and most pressing need, he felt, was to develop techniques for studying and analyzing in a scientific manner the problems of the schools. Second, he was concerned with the lack of civic pride in rural communities. In his view the rural community had to be encouraged to accept leadership roles in school affairs so that reforms could be accomplished from within the community rather than from sources external to the community. The third basic difficulty resulted from the general unfitness of the rural school buildings. "Until country schoolhouses are made so that they can be properly heated, ventilated, lighted," he said, "until they are provided with proper furniture and equipment, there isn't much use in endeavoring to get better teachers or better courses of study."

The fourth factor which he considered important was the teacher. In his opinion the country school teacher needed to be properly prepared for country school teaching rather than city school work. Both men and women were needed in the country schools and salaries needed to be raised in order to encourage teachers to accept positions in the rural schools.

Three years later (1912), Elliott reported to the N. E. A. Council on Education that perhaps the most important problem of all was the lack of financing for rural schools. Putting it simply, he said, "The problem of rural school improvement is one of rural school funds."

In January 1915, Cubberley and Elliott had an article published in *School and Society* on rural school administration. These two friends had just completed their book, *State and County School Administration,* and the magazine article was a direct result of this work. It was the last published statement by Elliott on the rural school problem and indicated that his ideas had changed considerably from those espoused six years earlier.

Since both Elliott and Cubberley had been working in the field of administration they felt that a "thoroughly fundamental reorganization of rural education, along the lines of the best city administration experience," would be required before country children could have an education as good as that provided for children in the cities. They felt that rural schools needed (1) larger administrative units, (2) reorganization and consolidation, and (3) a nonpolitical superintendent, with secondary emphasis on (4) a new-type teacher and (5) a reorganized curriculum. Whereas the 1909 articles stressed the importance of local leadership, stating that "the real reform of the rural school situation must come not from *without* but from *within,*" the 1915 article said "the necessary reorganizations will have to be superimposed from above . . . . The state . . . must demand a reorganization of rural education . . . ." The ideal of reform remained the same, but the method of reaching the ideal represented a direct switch in thinking.

Cubberley, of course, published many books in later years on school administration and came to be known as one of the foremost authorities in the field. It is not widely known, however, that Cubberley and Elliott had made ambitious plans to co-author a number of texts in administration.

An understanding had been reached with the Macmillan Company to publish four volumes, two as a part of a textbook series in education, and two as a part of a source book series in education. The first to be published (in 1914) was Cubberley's *State and County Educational Reorganization,*[7] which mentioned the three volumes to follow: *Principles of State and County School Administration,* by Cubberley and Elliott; *A Source Book in State and County School Administration,* by Cubberley and Elliott; and *Selected Legal Decisions Relating to Education,* by Elliott.

In 1915, the source book was published, but the following year Elliott left the teaching field to become chancellor of the University of Montana. The same year (1916), Cubberley was engaged by the Houghton Mifflin Company to edit a new series called the Riverside Textbooks in Education. Cubberley's first book in that series, *Public School Administration,* made numerous references to *Principles of State and County School Administration* by Cubberley and Elliott, and *Legal Decisions Relating to Education* by Elliott, both of which he listed as published by the Macmillan Company in 1916. Interested readers who attempted to find these two references were surely confused, for neither of the books was ever published! While Cubberley continued to publish for many years in the field of public school administration, Elliott became an administrator in higher education who could find little time to author many of the books which he had planned earlier.

The proposed book on legal decisions was undoubtedly to be based on his earlier studies of legislation prepared for the U. S. Bureau of Education. While this volume was never completed, nearly twenty years later (in 1934), Elliott and Chambers published *Charters and Basic Laws of Selected American Universities and Colleges,* and (in 1936) the first of a series entitled *The Colleges and the Courts.* While the subject had changed from public school administration to that of higher education, the basic idea had remained essentially the same.

THE SUPERINTENDENT AS
EDUCATIONAL EXPERT

The early part of the century witnessed a period of extraordinary development in education which required educators to reexamine their ideals. In reviewing those Elliott papers which considered the superintendent and his part in controlling the schools, for example, it is possible to trace the growth and development of a part of his philosophy.

At Leadville, Superintendent Elliott had had practically unlimited control. The board of education had followed his suggestions with enthusiasm and his policies had generally received support from teachers and parents. To explain his position, as early as 1901 Elliott had written that the superintendent "is to be the educational expert, upon whom the progress of our schools and the solution of their problems is to devolve." There is little evidence that teachers, patrons, or board members had any hand in forming school policies at Leadville. Elliott clearly felt that the people were obligated to delegate power and responsibility "from untechnical laymen to the technical experts."

At Wisconsin in 1907, Elliott was disturbed that the public schools were at that time controlled and indirectly operated by laymen. "This form of control and operation has resulted in getting the machines into the hands of the unskilled, the untechnical, the empirical hands that have preferred the lever of expediency," he wrote, "rather than that of projected, intelligent policy." He complained that "everybody feels competent to execute and direct operations."

Elliott felt that there were many school superintendents, however, who were not adequately prepared and not qualified as a technical expert. He noted that the school superintendent should be prepared to train teachers who were "potentially, but not actually, competent." "To be able to *make* one effective teacher from an ineffective teacher," he wrote, "is trebly more indicative of professional skill than to be able to select and employ three already effective teachers." He must have raised more than a few eyebrows when he stated that "the present mode of administration and supervision, especially as existing and influencing the schools of the small or medium-sized cities and rural communities, cannot be characterized as expert in skill."

Not until several years later was Elliott willing to admit that persons other than the superintendents should have a voice in school affairs. In 1910, however, he surmised that there was some justification for "a partial initiation of the teacher into the dominant educational ideals of this democracy of ours" and thus give him an acquaintanceship with the "governing principles of organization that make our school mechanism what it is." At the same time he was disturbed that "the duly selected lay officials, the teachers in the ranks, the journalists of regular or irregular standing, the parent, the specialist in any profession, the 'ologist in any field, yea, even at times the pupils; each feels himself or herself competent to grasp one of the controlling levers of this vast social engine of education."

There were a number of experiences in the years that followed which led Elliott to rework and modify somewhat his philosophy regarding the control of public schools. Without question, one of these experiences was his work on the New York School Inquiry in 1911 which will be reviewed in another section. Evidence of this change of viewpoint appeared in 1912 when Elliott wrote a chapter entitled "Instruction: Its Organization and Control" for Charles H. Johnston's book, *High School Education*. In this essay he outlined a plan for school control which included boards of education but still gave the final responsibility to the superintendent and placed the teacher in an advisory capacity.

As he analyzed the chief controlling forces of the public schools, he noted that there were four distinct elements: the legislative, the administrative, the supervisory, and the inspectorial. Legislative control he defined as that form of regulation centered in the legislature, by whose sanction "all public schools owe their existence, derive their support, and carry on their work . . ." Administrative control was vested in the agencies created by legislative action such as boards of education, boards of trustees, and their employees such as superintendents and inspectors. Supervisory control depended upon individuals who possessed technical and expert knowledge of educational processes, while inspectorial control had as its purpose provision of impersonal, objective measurement of the results and worth of the school.

According to Elliott, the responsibility of the supervisors and inspectors included the development of the curriculum, the right and responsibility of selecting the textbooks, and the right to select the teachers. These responsibilities were under no circumstances to be assumed by the agencies of legislative or administrative control.

When Elliott's report on the New York School Inquiry, *City School Supervision*, was published in 1914, it repeated his four distinct elements of the controlling forces of the school. One of his main criticisms of the New York system was that there seemed to be no "clear and conscious discrimination between those activities of control that are administrative in character and those that are supervisory or inspectorial."

He still reacted strongly against lay control of instruction but his recommendations asked that teachers be given a voice in school control since "a school system cannot teach, cannot vitalize democracy with children free and teachers in chains."

Ten years before at Leadville, Elliott had made no recommendations to give the "enchained teachers" a place in school control, although he had worked diligently to raise salaries and provide tenure.

At about the time that Elliott was concluding his work at Wisconsin, his ideas on school control had been modified still further to include the teachers and the members of the community in which the school was located.

In a speech before the Minnesota Educational Association he said, "The school is governed best that requires the principal the least . . . (for) the dynamic center of the school is the teacher . . . . Every school ought to be controlled by its teachers. I am not certain but what sooner or later we are coming to the point where the teachers are to elect their own principals," he continued, "and I am not certain but what teachers are going to elect a superintendent of schools."

Sometime later in an address before the Wisconsin Teacher's Association he said, "The present scheme of school government by school boards and school superintendents is apparently designed to secure the least rather than the most service from teachers." He further noted that both teachers and pupils should be included in the conception of a free public school.

Almost imperceptibly through the years from 1898 to 1914, there was a change in outlook. And the change that took place in Elliott's thinking was the change that came over the entire educational reform movement. The leaders submitted themselves and their methods to scientific analysis and tried to accept what they found with scientific detachment. "Democracy" in education was the word used freely at the beginning of the century, but it took workers and thinkers like Cubberley, Thorndike, Strayer, and Elliott to make the public schools more nearly democratic and still retain the guidance of experts.

THE SCHOOL SURVEY

The school survey movement, which developed during this period, was an important step forward in the trend toward the scientific study of education. Cubberley,[8] Knight,[9] and Sears[10] have prepared accounts of the early work in the survey movement, and all have mentioned the early surveys in Montclair (1911), Baltimore (1911), Boise (1912), and New York (1911-1912). Elliott was a member of two of these early survey commissions, each of which helped to shape later school survey procedures.

While it is sometimes extremely difficult to isolate and attempt to trace an idea, there are certain guideposts in Elliott's background which seem to point toward his eventual participation in the school survey movement. His series of articles relating to the problems of the rural school situation was his first direct reference to the need for an expert study of schools. It seems clear that his interest in school surveys was a later development of some of these ideas.

Even though there was much evidence that many reforms were to be forthcoming in the nation's schools, educational reformers as yet had proceeded in a somewhat disorganized manner. Areas which apparently needed study were being discovered at random, and a haphazard array of remedies were proposed in special areas with little regard for areas of greatest need. To Elliott and some of his contemporaries it soon became evident that a diagnosis had to be made before solutions to problems in education could be properly advanced. As a scientist, Elliott felt it was obvious that scientific tools and techniques had to be provided before the study and analysis of schools could proceed in an appropriate manner.

In October 1909, Elliott pointed out in an article in the *Educational Review* the four stages of educational reform as "the stage of stress and pressure, the stage of investigation, the stage of propaganda, and the stage of application and reorganization." He was ready for the second stage.

The first city school survey participated in by Elliott was the New York City Inquiry. This intensive statistical study was made under the direction of Paul Hanus, a professor of education at Harvard from 1891 to 1921. The results of the study, edited by Hanus, were published by the World Book Company as the *School Efficiency Series* and consisted of twelve volumes by as many educational experts and consisted of monographs based on the report of Hanus and his associates on the schools of New York City. Elliott's contribution to this series was *City School Supervision.*

According to Elliott, Hanus was particularly bitter (and somewhat profane) in his estimates of the entire survey. In 1937, he published an article in the *Harvard Educational Review* which explained his experience in directing this survey of the largest public school system in the country.[11] "Other large cities have had school surveys," he said, "but none of them, so far as I know, was so obliquely originated, or had to be carried on under such persistent and harrassing obstructions from persons outside the school systems as fell to the lot of the New York survey."

Elliott had his shares of difficulties, too, but the indignities suffered came largely from the press and from members of the New York school system who had received a share of the criticisms. In retrospect, however, it becomes apparent that Elliott gained prestige and information from this experience which provided him with material for several published contributions to education.

Elliott's first reports were severely critical of the administration and supervision of the New York schools. He had recommended a general reorganization which included the abolition of the board of superintendents, the creation of a supervisory council, the establishment of a bureau of investigation and appraisal, and the reorganization of the board of examiners.

Elliott's report touched some tender spots and the board of superintendents complained that while his report might appear to be sound and reasonable, it was "inconsistent and misleading, and unfair and unjust in its conclusion."

When the board published a review and reply to the Hanus-Elliott report it included approximately twenty pages of specific facts on Elliott and the Elliott report then concluded petulantly, "Professor Elliott fails to show in his report any adequate realization of the magnitude and complexity of the system and of the efforts that are necessary to keep pace with its growth." Continuing, the reply noted that "the writer is evidently biased and the information on which the report is based is incomplete and inaccurate." The report concluded that "it was not expected that either Professor Hanus or Professor Elliott could thoroughly appreciate the many phases of school work presented by the city of New York, a city that is unique in the vastness and variety of the problems which it is called upon to solve, but it was expected that the investigators would approach the problems in a professional spirit and with a slight recognition, at least, of some accomplishments on the part of the board of superintendents."

While the newspaper comments on the survey dealt largely with details of major importance, at least on one occasion, they reported an attack of a petty, personal nature. The *New York Press,* on June 15, 1912, printed this item:

> Controller Prendergast said yesterday that although he is eager that the city pay its pressing bills as quickly as they can be proved, he will not pay for the pressing of the trousers of members of commissions appointed to make investigations for the city. He turned back a bill of Professor Edward C. Elliott of Madison, Wisconsin, one of the School Board Inquiry Commission, one of his reasons being that it has a charge of sixty cents for pressing the Professor's trousers.

A few days later, however, the *New York American* came to the defense of Elliott and the Commission with an editorial:

> The *New York World* [apparently most of the papers picked up this item] is excited because a charge of pressing Professor Edward C. Elliott's trousers somehow got into that gentlemen's expense account against the city. Professor Elliott is one of the educational specialists who for some months have been working for the city with Professor Paul H. Hanus of Harvard and other educators of high reputation—trying to discover, by a searching investigation of the city's whole vast school system, how the city may get larger returns for the million dollars a week that it spends for the upkeep of the schools.
>
> Considering the very economical basis on which this important commission of inquiry is being conducted and the immense size of its work, the *American* thinks that the creases in Professor Elliott's trousers ought to be waived. If, however, the *World* insists upon waving the trousers, we do not believe that any large portion of the people of New York will salute or follow the *World's* banner of discontent.

The final paragraph of the editorial concluded that people in the New York City community should recognize that many "small politicians and petty grafters who have some kind of private interest in the maintenance of the ancient futilities and abuses will disapprove of every part of the survey report."

In spite of all that was written to discredit the work of the New York survey, it was, nevertheless, an important piece of work.

Hanus, Elliott, and the others were pioneering to establish new methods and techniques of investigation. The school survey movement was on its way.

One other personal incident occurred in New York that affected the entire family. Elliott had just finished teaching a summer session class at the University of Chicago in August 1911, and went directly to New York to begin the survey work. After only a few weeks in that city he realized that he was not feeling as well as he should so he went to the hospital for a check up. The doctors there ordered him to go home as fast as he could.

He endured a miserable train ride to Madison, was met at the station by his local doctor, and went straight to the hospital where his illness was diagnosed as typhoid fever.

It was the first time he had ever been sick, but he was forced to spend four months convalescing, not teaching for the entire first semester.

It was a harrowing experience for the Elliott family. They had just recently built their home in Madison and there were two small children to look after (John was three and Susanne not a year old). Not only was it a severe financial blow, but it was a tremendous responsibility to place on Mrs. Elliott. Although Elliott was too sick to worry during the first weeks, he spent many restless weeks recovering, impatient, anxious to get up and get things done.

When he at last was on his feet, his work began again as usual. His health never failed again until his final illness.

The experience may have intensified his compulsion for "keeping in shape." Although he was bothered from time to time in later years by a chronic sinus condition, he rarely complained of not feeling well and seemed never to miss a day at work because of illness. Ed remembered also that his dad was not too sympathetic with any member of the family when anyone was sick; "He thought we could have avoided it by 'not getting run down' or by being 'more careful about diet'," Ed wrote later.

The following year (1912), upon invitation of the superintendent and board, a survey of the Boise, Idaho, public school system was made by Elliott, Judd, and George Strayer, then professor of educational administration at Teachers College. The conclusions were related to course of study, supervisory staff, teaching staff, school plant, school expenditures, and community cooperation. In addition a special report on instruction was made by Elliott.

In 1913 the Portland, Oregon, survey was made under the direction of Cubberley of Stanford University. Assisting Cubberley were Elliott, Lewis M. Terman, professor of education at Stanford, and others. The Portland report was prepared primarily for the people of the city, but Hanus and the World Book Company felt that the published report should be included in the *School Efficiency Series*. Accordingly, in 1915 *The Portland Survey* was published. Elliott's sections of the book dealt with "Census and Attendance" and "Records and Reports."

Also in 1913, Elliott, Milo B. Hillegas, professor of education at Teachers College, and William S. Learned, newly appointed assistant secretary of the Carnegie Foundation for the Advancement of Teaching, and others made a survey of the Vermont state school system. Sponsored by the Carnegie Foundation at the request of an educational commission which had been created to inquire into the needs of that state, the Vermont inquiry was the first survey made by a group that traveled over the state, basing its report on the result of its on-the-site examination.

Elliott helped plan the survey and made special studies of the normal schools and the state system of educational administration and expenditure. Hillegas studied the elementary schools while Learned examined the secondary schools.

Howard J. Savage, in his history of the Carnegie Foundation, reported that the work of the Division of Educational Inquiry of the Carnegie Foundation began with the study of education in Vermont.[12] He noted that "Professor Edward C. Elliott of Wisconsin, experienced in similar work, was engaged early" to help plan and carry out the state survey. In reviewing the work of the survey committee, Savage wrote that the Vermont study had four major characteristics: "simplicity of the report as addressed to laymen; diplomatic temper; the number of its conclusions, four only; and recommendations, only fifty-two in contrast with the hundreds, even thousands, in other similar enterprises." There was general agreement that the survey was sympathetically done yet was searching, detailed, and based upon much visiting and a wealth of accumulated data.

Perhaps the most widely known survey in these early days which involved Elliott, however, was the so-called Allen survey of the University of Wisconsin which was referred to earlier in the chapter. Elliott was not engaged in making the university survey, of course, but when the findings were released, he was forced into a period of feverish activity to refute and disprove the report submitted by Allen.

Thus Elliott learned at first hand in those early days both how to make a survey that could be genuinely helpful, and how not to make a survey. With these kinds of experiences behind him, it could have been anticipated that Elliott would also have an active part in later years in surveys which related to higher educational institutions and state systems for higher education.

In 1914, Elliott took time to organize his thoughts on school surveys, published two articles and delivered a major address on that subject. He pointed out that "this latest and delightfully disturbing form of educational activity—the school survey—is with us to remain; for awhile at least . . . ." He observed that a properly conducted school survey was not an investigation and should not have as its aim an attempt to bring individuals to trial; it was not to be used as a weapon for the settlement of personal feuds, factional controversies, or partisan warfare. He summarized the purposes of the school survey as "the accurate and comprehensive informing of the public as to the organization, administration, supervision, cost, physical equipment, teaching staff, methods and extent of instruction, and the achievement of teaching in the school system or educational institution." He had concluded that a public school survey should be "the public inventorying of educational resources and liabilities. It should be bigger and better than any man or set of men . . . ."

In 1937, Walter C. Eells referred to the articles quoted above in his book, *Surveys of American Higher Education*.[13] As he traced the development of the survey movement, Eells said, "the distinction between the 'survey' with its constructive implications, and the 'investigation' with its implication of agitation of the gadfly type was brought out . . . vigorously by Dr. Edward C. Elliott . . . in 1914."

Even at this early date in the survey movement, the appraisals made by Elliott show a keen awareness of its shortcomings as well as a deep appreciation of the value of the technique.

OTHER INTERESTS

During the years from 1897, the year he started teaching science in the Leadville High School, to 1916, the year he became chancellor of the University of Montana, Elliott was an eloquent and frequent champion of the public school system.

He was maturing in the midst of a tremendous growth of sentiment directed in favor of the public school. The early twentieth century saw intense interest in practically all areas of public education—support and control, curriculum, teacher training, and many others. The professional educators, fighting to achieve status and recognition, were generally concerned with the so-called scientific method as applied to education. Leaders were calling for investigations into a variety of problems of education in order to plan for the eventual reform of the public school system.

A glance at the selected bibliography (see appendix) gives some indication of Elliott's immense vitality and wide range of interests. Filled with ambition, he prepared and published nearly a hundred papers and reports during this period.

When the *Cyclopedia of Education* appeared in 1911 (edited by Paul Monroe), for example, Elliott had provided ten articles on a range of topics that included: appointment of teachers, city school administration, recent American educational commissions, sex of teachers, school board conventions, and teachers' pensions.

Many of his writings were clumsy, not polished or skillfully finished work. In striving for precision he frequently bogged down in phrases; a single sentence in one article, for example, involved 184 words. But he soon developed a more concise style and his articles became more readable. As he gained confidence, he relaxed enough to display his inherent sense of humor and perfected the overly ornate alliterative style which characterized some of his early writings.

Scarcely an area of study existed which did not, for a time at least, seem to catch Elliott's attention. One area of interest which claimed a portion of Elliott's time was the field of state legislation relating to public education. Elmer Ellsworth Brown, the new United States Commissioner of Education in 1906, as one of his first official acts, requested that Elliott, whom he had never met, prepare a digest of recent school legislation. Brown reasoned that the framers and promoters of bills dealing with the several state systems of education, as well as members of the state legislatures who were called on to vote on these bills, would welcome a publication which would record the precedents set in the recent school legislation of other states. It is likely Elliott was recommended to Brown by Cubberley, who had worked with both men at Stanford.

Two years earlier, a digest of the school laws of the several states had been published by the Bureau of Education as a part of the report of the commissioner of education for 1904. Elliott's compilation brought the earlier publication down to 1906, and included a carefully compiled and classified list of the recent educational enactments. A similar volume was issued at the close of the biennium 1907-08 entitled *State School Systems II: Legislative and Judicial Decisions Relating to Public Education.*

A third such bulletin was prepared by Elliott in 1910. In that publication, Brown explained that the two preceding biennial digests had proved their usefulness and had been very much in demand so that the digest would henceforth be published annually. He explained that although Elliott's work in this field had been universally recognized, it had been difficult to accomplish since Elliott was not located at all close to the office of publication. Although complimentary reviews reflected credit on both Brown and Elliott, Brown announced similar compilations in the future would be prepared in Washington by members of his staff.

As a result of the bulletin which appeared in 1906, Elliott was asked by the New York State Education Department to prepare a similar study of legislation for 1907-1908. In this publication, Elliott commented that "an analysis of the educational legislation enables the determination of many of the more significant tendencies in our social progress." He noted that the state offices of public instruction were taking steps to insure that schoolhouses were safe and sanitary; that legislatures were giving attention to the status of teachers and were increasing the amount of compensation for all school personnel; that steps were being taken to provide for better administration at both the state and local level; that most states were becoming more liberal with their appropriations for higher educational institutions; and that the federal government was moving to become a large and direct influence upon the general educational system.

Partly as a result of these highly successful reviews of legislation, particularly with regard to legislation which had been passed by the Congress of the United States, Elliott's attention was directed to the role of the federal government in education. While the issue of federal aid to education was not a particularly live one in the early 1900's, consideration was being given to the place of the federal government in public education at the elementary and secondary levels. Elliott could readily see that the bureau of education was in a position to exert tremendous influence in educational affairs. Here was an agency to originate and direct many investigations which would benefit the entire system of schools.

In the series of articles relating to rural school problems which he published in 1909, Elliott suggested that the federal government should perhaps establish "educational experiment stations". He reasoned that it would be helpful if the federal government would set up a model consolidated school in each state; such an expenditure would be as legitimate as the expenditure of federal funds for the establishment of agricultural experiment stations.

Although he mentioned the idea again in 1912 in an address before the National Education Association, the proposal was of a tentative nature and he did not pursue it with any great enthusiasm. The idea gained little support and, as a result, no public mention of the scheme was subsequently made by him.

On other occasions, however, he noted that many of the educational needs could be met "most directly and most effectively by the national government." He felt that the bureau of education should be "endowed with power and provided with resources for conducting in a scientific manner investigations of some of the larger and more important problems of education as they appear at the present time [1909], especially those problems that are concerned with elementary and secondary education." In his view the bureau of education should be expanded so that it could serve as the center for research in American education and thereby assume the responsibility of leadership. To Elliott, this was the greatest opportunity for service by the federal government.

In 1902 at Leadville, Elliott had asked that manual training courses be added to the curriculum. At the time he was not particularly impressed with the importance of job training in the public school, but he strongly favored the provision of some of the recognized forms of manual training (woodworking for the boys, cooking and sewing for the girls) since these courses were "most instrumental for individual development."

Six years later, as director of the Course for the Training of Teachers, Elliott urged that efforts be made to train special teachers in the areas of agriculture and manual training.

At the same time he observed that it was difficult for the public school to train workers for specific fields of industry because at that time it was difficult, if not impossible, to determine the extent of the demand for these kinds of industrial workers. Before he would be willing to encourage public schools to provide specific training functions, he thought that reliable data should be accumulated upon which a training program could be based.

In 1909, Elliott was asked to prepare a legislative summary for the American Association for Labor Legislation similar to the studies prepared for Commissioner Brown. This compilation was, however, a classified summary of existing legislation relative to industrial education in the public school. The following year Elliott, with C. A. Prosser, deputy commissioner of education in Massachusetts, prepared a similar bulletin for the American Association for Labor Legislation and the National Society for the Promotion of Industrial Education.

Elliott indicated that he had not been particularly interested in doing this work for the American Association for Labor Legislation but he had been urged to do so by John R. Commons, the noted labor economist and historian. Commons was twelve years older than Elliott but had come to the University of Wisconsin in 1904. They were good friends, both interested in industrial education, and it was Commons who brought Prosser and Elliott together to work on this second project. It was the last paper on industrial education that Elliott prepared, however.

Even though Elliott was rather completely occupied with the broad problems of policy and management of educational activities, he found that many of the specific details involved in the administration of public schools also claimed his attention. He was concerned, for example, with the school building and its uses in the community. In the early days at Leadville Elliott constantly hammered away at the board members and school patrons to establish a clean, efficient physical plant. He succeeded in getting a new high school building erected, but his last report showed clearly that there was much to be done before the superintendent would call all of the facilities even adequate.

Even though Elliott was never entirely preoccupied with the importance of an adequate physical plant, he kept returning to the subject, and the matter of proper buildings and equipment consistently received his attention. When he considered the rural school problem during the course of his work at Wisconsin, he invariably mentioned the need for properly heated, ventilated, lighted schoolhouses provided with proper furniture and equipment. He was largely responsible for erection of the new building to house Wisconsin High School and, at the time he left the university, he was calling for a "physical center about which the distinctive activities relating to the preparation of teachers could be organized and given a definite professional unity." He wanted a building to house the department of education to help the profession gain prestige, and to develop "craft consciousness" among the student teachers.

Elliott also came to visualize the school as a community center. This larger concept of the school was certainly developed over a period of several years with its beginning in Leadville. Elliott recalled that his first experience with a part of the community school concept came about in Leadville when a group of stationary engineers came to the new superintendent asking for information about boiler compounds. "I was presumptuous—a fool to attempt to teach these men something about boiler compounds," he said; but he went to Boulder, got some books on the subject, and gave a series of lectures at their request. As this was a successful venture, the local YMCA was encouraged to sponsor a course, "Everyday Chemistry," which Elliott conducted.

These activities were not considered a part of the work of the public school system. The school buildings were closed when the pupils left in the afternoon. If Elliott chose to accept an invitation to teach an evening class of adults, the board members tolerated it. There was nothing to indicate that the superintendent made any effort to expand the Leadville schools to serve the total adult community, although Elliott did more on his own than he might have been expected to do.

It was not until 1912 that Elliott wrote or spoke publicly on the community school. That year he was asked by E. J. Ward, a University of Wisconsin Extension Division staff member, to write a reply to the question, "In what ways is it possible for the public school social center movement to contribute to the improvement of those activities which the school regularly undertakes in the performance of its duty of educating children?" The question was a timely one because at that time a number of agencies and organizations concerned with education were discussing the use of the school as a community center.

Elliott's reply was printed as a chapter in a book, *The Social Center*, edited by Ward. "The magnified school" as Elliott chose to call this new school concept, was a place where teachers, parents, the artisans and the merchants could come together. "The Parent-Teacher Organizations which are now becoming more general throughout the country," he observed, "represent a move in the right direction." His Episcopalian background was apparent when he wrote that all adults in the community should help the school "do that which should be done, and leave undone those things which should not be done."

The following year Elliott prepared an address called "The Schoolhouse As A Crime Contributor" which was presented before the annual meeting of The American Academy of Medicine in Minneapolis in which he expanded some of the ideas expressed in "the magnified school." It was an entertaining talk, very well received, and contributed to his growing reputation as a speaker. To explain his title he said, "the specific charge brought against the modern schoolhouse is that of contributory negligence." He was disturbed that school personnel and adults in the community had not used the school to provide for the normal demands for activity on the part of both children and adults.

"The schoolhouse," he said, "must provide, within and without, for proper play space for the children of the neighborhood. This schoolhouse must constitute itself a center for the physical and social activities of the children outside as well as inside the the school." He continued, "The schoolhouse that keeps bankers' hours is only half a school . . . . The American schoolhouse must be constructed so as to enable its use as a common meeting place for the discussion of political problems and social issues. 'Keeping the school out of politics' is a pernicious doctrine." From this time on Elliott was an ardent champion of the expanded school. He came to visualize the public school, and the university as well, as a place for community service.

During his years at Leadville and to a much greater extent at Wisconsin, Elliott was called on from time to time to write book reviews for educational journals and other publications. He also learned to prepare press releases in order to get newspaper coverage for the various programs and activities in which he participated or directed.

By 1916, Elliott had become a skilled speaker, forceful, dynamic, with a deft sense of humor. He had an abundant supply of natural vigor and a strong, heavy voice, although he had no formal training in speech. He learned, as he recalled, by watching his audiences, making sure that he was heard by everyone, and by developing a keen sensitivity to audience reaction.

A complete listing of his public speeches is not possible to obtain, of course, but the selected bibliography lists all major addresses. His first shaky experience was as high school valedictorian in North Platte, orating on the topic, "The Value of a Liberal Education."

Because he spoke infrequently at Leadville, he was almost totally unprepared for the tremendous demand for addresses which came at Wisconsin. In 1907, he began a long series of high school commencement addresses with two engagements. The title of his address was "The Making of a Politician," an address which he used at least six times in subsequent commencements. These included addresses at Pueblo, Colorado, in 1909 and Milwaukee in 1912. A favorite commencement address was called "The Job Getters" and was used as the basis for more than a dozen speeches; another topic frequently used was "The Common Man and The Common School." The only time he ever returned to Leadville after leaving in 1903 was to deliver the commencement address in 1910.

The year 1907 also saw him start the rounds as an institute speaker. From 1907 to 1915 he spoke before more than thirty-five teacher organizations from Baltimore, Maryland, to Spokane, Washington. He was principal speaker at institutes in Maryland, Wisconsin, Minnesota, Michigan, Colorado, Idaho, Kansas, Ohio, Indiana, Kentucky, Iowa, Illinois, Montana, Missouri, Pennsylvania, South Dakota, and Washington.

The most popular and most frequently used address was his talk on the rating scale for measuring teacher merit. It was variously entitled "The Measurement of Efficiency of Teachers," "Standards For Judging the Efficiency of Teachers," "Measuring the Efficiency of Teachers," "What Are the Measures of a Teachers' Real Worth?" and, most frequently, "The Measure of Merit of Teachers." He gave this address on more than twenty occasions in all parts of the country, and his reputation as a speaker continued to grow.

THE STATE UNIVERSITY

Of all of the many areas which claimed Elliott's attention, the one most fully developed in later years was the consideration given to the role and responsibilities of the state university.

As has been pointed out, Elliott worked rather closely with Van Hise as a liaison between the president and the state superintendent of schools. The relationship was a constant one from 1905 to 1916. As the Department of Education gradually began to assume leadership also during those years, the Course for the

Training of Teachers further emphasized professional training in educational methods.

The trend toward an increased number of "education courses" indicates that Van Hise gradually began to accept many of Elliott's plans for the professional training of teachers. At the same time, of course, Elliott was absorbing much of the president's philosophy regarding the state university. There was considerable mutual admiration, and the two served each other well.

A study of Elliott's interests in the administration of higher education may begin with a convocation address which he gave at the 1910 commencement exercises at the University of Idaho. Even in his undergraduate days at Nebraska he had shown an interest in university affairs (he clipped several of Chancellor Canfield's addresses for his scrapbook), but he had written nothing to demonstrate this interest. Here, then, for the first time were recorded his ideas relating to the state university. On one occasion Elliott told me, "I believe that in this address I developed some of the more important concepts of my entire career."

For the most part the ideas represent an acknowledgment of the contributions of Van Hise, but Elliott worked hard on this address to give an analysis of his own philosophy of higher education. "The history of the development of American education," he said, "may be summed up in the one word, *equity*—that no individual, whatever be his station in life, shall be without the circle of influence of the free education, erected and supported by the state—the people. . . . ."

> The establishment of the state universities represented the first step in the democratizing, the universalizing of an education beyond the steps of the elementary and high school . . . . The college, under the old regime, and the first universities, under the new order of public education, endeavored to perform a single function —the teaching of orthodox, formal, wordy truth, as the teachers understood the truth, to those students who came within their walls. This had been the way of the educational world since the days of the medieval college and university. Commencing four or more decades ago there was added as a result of the development of the natural sciences, together with the new situations created by economic pressure of various kinds, a second function—that of increasing, through experiment, study, and investigation, the store of the world's truth. The agricultural experiment stations in connection with our agricultural colleges are the most familiar exemplifications of this expansion of the activity and responsibility of the university . . . .

To the ordinary functions of teaching student youth and of scientific investigation has been added a third, which for want of a better name, I shall designate as *service*. Even thus early there are signs that this third great activity will not only rank with the other two, but is likely to transcend them in point of actual realization of the principles of public education among the democratic people. "We say today that the ideal of the state university is that it shall be co-extensive with the state" is the true expression of President Charles R. Van Hise, of the University of Wisconsin, a conspicuous leader of the new movement, in defining its significance.

[T]he agricultural college and experiment station as educational and investigating institutions early discovered the limitations imposed upon their efficiency by academic traditions. A new form of educational pioneering had to be undertaken. Instead of expecting students to come to them, they had to betake themselves to the students. Thus developed an educational machinery of a distinctive type, which included the Farmer's Institute, the demonstration farms, short courses of instruction, popular, scientific bulletins, etc. These and other similar undertakings have become a part and parcel of the truly progressive American agricultural and mechanical college. It may be safely asserted that of all the educational establishments created by the modern democratic state, the agricultural institutions have best served to demonstrate the means and possibilities of the newer higher education.

The problem which our higher educational institutions are now facing is to discover ways and means for rendering service to those engaged in the other major industrial activities. The miner, the lumberman, the merchant, the machinist, the banker, the bookkeeper, are as much entitled as the agriculturist to share in the benefits of the best of modern economic skill, knowledge, and insight. . . .

No state university that purposes to assume its full duties dares longer to neglect the man or woman who desires to share in the trust fund of vitalized knowledge which is productive skill. . . . This seems to me fully to express the idea behind the larger university movement: to make education a part of the daily practical occupation of all the people of the state; and to make the university independent of place, of party, of class; and to cause the university to do that which the forceful and farseeing president of the University of Wisconsin says it should do, "to take up any line of educational work within the state for which the university is the best fitted instrument!"

It was probably not a mere coincidence that the trustees made an attempt to secure Elliott for the presidency of the University of Idaho just three years later in 1913; but Elliott at that time paid scant heed to the proposition.

As his interest in higher education developed, Elliott became more and more concerned with the relation of the state university to other parts of the system of public instruction; and even though he was rather deeply involved in many other troublesome issues, he found time to organize his philosophy to include the state university and its functions with regard to public service.

In November 1913, he spoke again on the topic of higher education before the Canadian Club of Winnipeg. The subject of the address was the university and public service, and his theme centered on the aspects of a university which could train the worker as well as give the professional man his start in life. "The most conspicuous problem of the modern state university," Elliott said, "is to discover ways and means of rendering service to the common people for the betterment of their daily life."

He repeated many of the concepts he had first expressed three years earlier at Idaho but concluded by saying "service to the state is no longer a matter of choice on the part of schools and universities . . . . It is the affair of the state to require that such service be rendered to the end that the people of the whole state may receive daily dividends from the knowledge, ability and opportunity which they have capitalized in these institutions. And from these dividends to secure for themselves a sounder physical life, a better economic order, a surer political progress and a highly ethical satisfaction."

"In the past the ebb of energy has been from the state to the university," he continued. "Today the flow is from the university to the state. This means the constant concentration of institutional efforts for the enlargement of opportunity, not for scholars and students alone, but for the combined citizenship of the commonwealth." Elliott developed these ideas at both the University of Montana and Purdue University.

As his interests widened, Elliott became more and more involved in the administration of higher education. Here was an outlet for his energy which offered some promise of freedom. Whereas the department of education at Wisconsin promised to settle into a well-defined pattern, he could see new areas unfolding in the field of higher education.

As he viewed the prospect of becoming an administrator in higher education, he was surely comforted by the knowledge that his background had provided a tremendously varied core of experiences. He had the friendship and support of the brightest names in education; prestige as an author and speaker; the experience of close contact with boards of control, legislators, students, and the people; plus immense vitality and physical strength.

Elliott was not ready to "settle down" in 1915, and he was not to be dissuaded when the opportunity came to go to Montana. The chancellorship was a challenge he wanted to accept.

Edward (right) and his brother Fred were photographed around 1878.

In North Platte, Nebraska, circa 1892, the Elliott family posed for a formal portrait. Left to right are Susan P. Elliott, Frederick, Jr., Edward, Frederick Elliott, and Benjamin.

After his first year of teaching in the Leadville, Colorado, schools Elliott came home to North Platte, Nebraska, for the summer of 1898. This snapshot was taken with his younger brother, Ben, and the family dog, Jack. Ben said there was always a dog around the home—always named Jack.

Elliott was a graduate student at Teachers College for two years (1903-04 and 1904-05) and spent the summer of 1904 at the University of Jena, Germany. This studio photo was taken in 1906, when he was thirty-one years old.

At the University of Wisconsin, Elliott was named first director of the course for the Training of Teachers in 1909. This portrait was taken in Madison about 1910, when Elliott was 35 years old.

The Purdue University Board of Trustees in June 1923 were, left to right: (back row) James W. Noel, Perry H. Crane, Mary M. Williams, John A. Hillenbrand, F. F. Chandler, David E. Ross; (front row) C. M. Hobbs, Mrs. Virginia C. Meredith, Joseph D. Oliver, President Edward C. Elliott, Henry W. Marshall.

During the Semi-Centennial
Celebration May 1924, left to
right were: President Edward
A. Birge, University of Wis-
consin, President Edward C.
Elliott, Purdue University,
President William O. Thomp-
son, Ohio State.

Elliott stood for an informal
picture outside Fowler Hall
in October 1924.

President Elliott's office in 1928 was in Fowler Hall, where this portrait was taken.

The president was given a new car by the Purdue Alumni Association in May 1929.

Elliott visited George Ade at Hazelden Farm (Brook, Indiana) in September 1929.

Charles H. Judd of the University of Chicago accepted Elliott's invitation to teach at Purdue during the 1930 summer session.

Elliott posed for a formal portrait at his desk in Fowler Hall in January 1932, during his 10th year as president of Purdue.

Elliott's portrait was presented to the University at the first Founders' Day Dinner, May 6, 1932, held to commemorate the 63rd anniversary of the founding of Pudue and to honor Elliott's first ten years at the University. James W. Noel, member of the Board of Trustees, unveiled the oil painting which was done by Robert W. Grafton, prominent Michigan City (Indiana) artist. It now hangs in the Edward C. Elliott Hall of Music.

Head table group at first Founder's Day dinner, May 6, 1932, from left to right were: W. O. Thompson, president emeritus, Ohio State University; Robert W. Grafton, Michigan City artist; O. M. Booher, executive secretary, Purdue Alumni Association; Fay F. Chandler, toastmaster; Walter Krull, president, Purdue Alumni Association; H. G. Leslie, governor, State of Indiana; David Ross, president, Board of Trustees; Elliott.

Amelia Earhart and Elliott discussed her proposed round-the-world flight in November 1935.

NOTES

1. H. H. Remmers and N. L. Gage, *Educational Measurement and Evaluation* (New York: Harper and Brothers, 1943), p. 129.

2. *Survey of the University of Wisconsin* (Madison, Wisconsin: State Board of Public Affairs, 1914).

3. George H. Mead, "Madison," *The Survey*, XXXV (December 25, 1915), pp. 349-51, 354-61.

4. Merle Curti and Vernon Carstensen, *The University of Wisconsin, 1848-1925* (Madison, Wisconsin: The University of Wisconsin Press, 1949) II, 257-8.

5. Simeon J. Domas and David V. Tiedeman, "Teacher Competence: An Annotated Bibliography," *The Journal of Experimental Education,* VII (March 1937), pp. 184-97.

6. Jesse B. Sears, "Measurement of Teaching Efficiency," *Journal of Educational Research,* IV (April 1921) 84.

7. Ellwood P. Cubberley, *State and County Educational Reorganization* (New York: The Macmillan Company, 1914).

8. ———, *Public School Administration* (Boston: Houghton Mifflin Company, 1916).

9. Edgar W. Knight, *Education in the United States* (Boston: Ginn and Company, 1929).

10. Sears, "The School Survey Movement," *Modern School Administration,* J. C. Almack, ed. (New York: Houghton Mifflin Company, 1933) pp. 217-59.

11. Paul Hanus, "An Early Survey of the Schools of a Great City," *Harvard Educational Review,* VII (March 1937), 184.

12. Howard J. Savage, *Fruit of an Impulse* (New York: Harcourt Brace and Company, 1953), p. 110.

13. Walter C. Eells, *Surveys of American Higher Education* (New York: The Carnegie Foundation for the Advancement of Teaching, 1937), p. 4.

CHAPTER 3

The University of Montana

"In 1916," Elliott said with a smile, "I gave up my scholarly activities and became a messenger boy for the boards of control." It was his off-hand way of describing a major career change that brought him face to face with a new set of issues, in another location, with different challenges, many requiring almost immediate solutions. He had accepted the newly-created position of chancellor of the University of Montana, a post that was unique among the systems of higher education in this country.

His work to this point had largely centered in the public schools. At Leadville, as at Madison, he had been concerned with the problems of pupils, teachers, parents, school buildings, and administrators. He had been a so-called "professional educator" engaged in research and teaching related to the training of public school teachers and administrators. Although he had had administrative responsibility, he had viewed himself as a professor of education, a scholar. His work with elementary and secondary schools had required little travel except as a lecturer or school survey staff member and most of his personal contacts were with other professors, students, teachers, and school administrators.

Embarking on what might be termed his fourth career, Elliott almost overnight found himself working primarily with college and university administrators and an endless variety of state officials, while traveling almost constantly over the wide ranges of Montana. He had almost no contact with students and their parents and he quickly found himself viewing a number of issues with a different perspective. He was no longer a colleague of the teaching and research staff members; and the problems associated with the administration of state colleges and universities, not the public schools, became paramount.

Many of his friends throughout the profession were considerably disturbed when they learned that Elliott was seriously considering leaving Wisconsin for Montana. Judd, for example, wrote from Chicago in response to a letter from Elliott, "I wish I could focus on you all the persuasion of all the Education people. It would be a unanimous opinion against your moving." Judd reported that he had talked with Cubberley and Abraham Flexner, then assistant secretary of the Carnegie Foundation, among others, and that they all wanted him to stay in education.

Another friend and colleague, philosophy professor A. O. Lovejoy of Johns Hopkins, wrote that the Montana situation was "exceedingly precarious." According to Lovejoy the system of organization of the boards of control was poor, there was an ongoing personal and political feud between two board members, other bitter rivalries existed, and, he concluded, "The governing boards in Montana have not yet learned to treat University officials with elementary decency."

Two friends, however, encouraged him to make the change. The most influential was Dean James Russell, his former professor at Teachers College, who wired, "Have been urging your election in Montana and believe it excellent opportunity to do great constructive work. Congratulations." The other was former classmate Henry Suzzalo, newly elected president of the University of Washington, who wrote, "All hail to you! A great success and a long career . . . . All your friends will be delighted to welcome you."

After several weeks of soul-searching, fact-finding, and negotiating, Elliott became convinced that the job offered him an exceptional opportunity to pioneer in the administration of higher education. "If successful," he wrote, "it should be of distinct influence in our American higher educational system; if it fails—why, of course, I am the victim either of circumstance or of my own inability."

A few days after Elliott had agreed to go to Montana (in October 1915) he wrote at some length to Russell from Wisconsin:

> "Practically all of my colleagues here frankly say to me that I am fool-hardy to the last degree. Of all my friends in the country who are in my estimation competent to advise me but two expressed a belief that it offers an opportunity. The first one of these was yourself. Suzzalo wrote me encouragingly, but it was natural of him to call out, 'Come on in. The water is fine!' So you see, you and I have pitted our judgments against all the rest of my advisors. I am anticipating my new work with pleasure and confi-

dence. I have carefully investigated the situation and believe that the task, however difficult, may be accomplished. Moreover, as I told Mrs. Elliott at a moment of indecision, that never yet had I missed anything by following your own advice."

To Lovejoy he wrote:

"Many of my friends think I am fool-hardy in assuming the new position. Notwithstanding the risks involved, I believe that such problems of the higher educational institutions of Montana can be solved best by making a careful, honest trial of such new plans as those represented by the Chancellorship."

To all of his friends Elliott indicated that he was leaving Wisconsin with great regret. He had established his family in Madison and had lived there longer than any other single place. "The roots of personal relationships are deeper here than elsewhere," he noted, but he was eager to try something new.

Many newspapers and magazines, of course, carried accounts of the election of Elliott to the chancellorship. In Wisconsin the reports emphasized the heavy loss to the state and an editorial in the *Wisconsin Journal of Education* acknowledged that it had required "tremendous insight, energy, persistence, and courage to accomplish the tasks of putting a course for the training of teachers on a par with other courses."

In Montana the newspapers contained glowing accounts of Elliott's accomplishments. Reporters secured copies of several letters sent to the governor of Montana and an article appeared in many papers over the state which quoted excerpts from these letters written by Cubberley; W. C. Bagley, head of the Department of Education, University of Illinois; Suzzalo; Strayer; Van Hise; Russell; Judd; and Lotus D. Coffman, dean of the Department of Education, University of Minnesota. They were unanimous in their support of Elliott for the chancellorship, after the decision had been made.

THE SITUATION IN MONTANA

The state of Montana, following the pattern set by many other states, had established four colleges and universities at four separate locations over the state in 1893. Because these four state institutions—The State School of Mines at Butte, The State College of Agriculture and Mechanical Arts at Bozeman, The State University at Missoula, and the Normal College at Dillon—were separately organized, competing with each other for appropriations, there had been constant pressure on the governor and the State Board of Education to clear up the unwieldy system that was expensive and created almost constant turmoil. Many people in the state felt that some plan had to be devised to eliminate the alleged waste, duplication, and competition which threatened to destroy the system of higher schools.

One faction had favored a single state university in one location to include the curriculum of all four schools, yet there was considerable opposition to this plan for none of the four cities wanted to lose its present school. One of the most ardent leaders of the movement for physical consolidation was Dr. E. B. Craighead, president of the State University at Missoula, who had argued that one state university would lead to economy in the administration of higher education in the state. Craighead eventually was dismissed (in 1915) because of his stand on consolidation.

At a meeting of the State Legislature in 1913, as a substitute plan, it was suggested that the four state schools be placed under a chancellor, appointed by the State Board of Education, with offices in the state capitol at Helena. As an educational experiment, the assembly approved the new plan.

There was delay in carrying out these provisions, but a second attempt at consolidation was voted down at a general election in November 1914. Then the next session of the legislature (1915) voted to repeal the law of 1913 setting up the chancellorship. Governor S. V. Stewart vetoed the bill, however, and the plans were definitely started to place the four schools under the unified management and administration of a chancellor of the State Collegiate Institutions.

It was a somewhat awkward arrangement that placed the institutions, each with a president, under a chancellor; but the people in Montana were generally optimistic concerning the new plan, and it was hoped that the new chancellor would be able to bring some order to the bitter, chaotic struggle which had gone before. The plan was generally approved in Bozeman, Dillon, and Butte, but there was still some opposition at Missoula.

Governor Stewart began the search for the new chancellor not long after the close of the legislative session of 1915. The recommendations from Teachers College led the Governor to begin negotiations with Elliott on August 7, 1915, and by the third week of September Elliott had arranged to visit with the State Board of Education in Helena. Elliott was pleased to learn that one of the board members, State Superintendent of Schools H. A. Davee, had been one of his students at Wisconsin and had urged other members of the board to give Elliott careful consideration.

Shortly after this visit Elliott wrote the governor that he was prepared to consider the matter formally if the board could furnish sound guarantees with regard to several matters. He specifically indicated ten conditions that would need to be met before he would agree to accept. These conditions stipulated, in part, that he receive a unanimous vote of the board along with the approval of the presidents and deans of the four educational institutions; that he be named to a three year term with an $8,000 beginning salary (twice the amount he was receiving in Wisconsin); that his term of service begin on February 1, 1916; and that provisions be made for an adequate office staff, travel expenses, vacation, and attendance at appropriate state and national education association meetings.

He also asked that the board pass a resolution committing itself in favor of the principle of providing tenure for the members of the faculties and that the chancellor be empowered to recommend all nominations for the appointment of new staff members as well as the compensation, promotion, or dismissal of staff members. It was further understood that he would not be expected to make any public addresses for at least six months after beginning his term of office.

As it turned out, these conditions, or understandings, worked so well that seven years later, when Elliott was considering moving to Indiana as president of Purdue University, he followed this same pattern by preparing a list of fourteen conditions for board approval.

The board accepted the proposals and the contract was signed on October 11, 1915. The arrangement was a challenge to Elliott's administrative skill and represented a major change for the state board; no other higher educational system in the nation was organized on quite the same basis.

During the weeks that followed, the governor and the new chancellor corresponded frequently to clear the way for the new administration. The governor was highly optimistic and completely confident that the new plan would work. His comments were heartening to Elliott and he became convinced that the governor and the board were resolved to fully "develop the higher educational system of the state."

But there were problems; and no small part of their correspondence related to a situation that had developed on the Missoula campus even before negotiations with Elliott were started.

In June 1915, three professors at the State University at Missoula were dismissed from the staff, allegedly at the insistence of a member of the State Board of Education. No reason was given for the abrupt discharge, and some members of the faculty became incensed at this summary treatment. The newly-organized American Association of University Professors was called in to investigate the alleged irregularity and to publish its findings.

By a fortunate circumstance, Elliott was in a better position to have a complete understanding of this situation than almost any other candidate whom the board might have selected. Months before he had even thought of going to Montana as chancellor, Elliott had become a charter member of the AAUP and his early association with that organization gave him a vantage point from which to examine the charges and countercharges.

THE AMERICAN ASSOCIATION OF UNIVERSITY PROFESSORS

The AAUP apparently had its genesis in 1913 when a committee was organized to explore the possibility of establishing a national association of professors. Elliott's first formal contact came late in 1914 when John Dewey, then a professor of philosophy at Columbia University, and A. O. Lovejoy, then a professor of philosophy at Johns Hopkins, wrote requesting Elliott's cooperation in this undertaking and asking him whether or not he could attend an organization meeting to be held in New York in January 1915. Elliott probably did not attend that meeting but in February 1915, after receiving a membership brochure, he sent in his annual dues and became a charter member of that organization.

Within three months AAUP's first president, John Dewey, had appointed Elliott a member of the Committee of Fifteen on Academic Freedom with E. R. Seligman, then a professor of political science at Columbia University, as chairman of this important group.

The Committee on Academic Freedom almost immediately was bombarded with letters from disgruntled professors from all parts of the country. It soon became apparent to committee members that some kind of plan had to be devised which would select only certain cases for investigation. Guy S. Ford, dean of the graduate school at the University of Minnesota and a member of the committee, wrote that the way cases were coming in, about one a week, the investigative tasks of the committee were going to have to be redefined. "We can hardly look up adequately every case," he said, "and those men we pass over and their friends will soon proclaim us inadequate and indifferent."

Without knowing of Ford's letter, Elliott sent a similar letter to Chairman Seligman confirming that there was a need for specific limitations on what the committee should attempt to do. He concluded his letter, referring to a specific case under discussion, by writing, "I am of the judgment that this case might well be taken up primarily for the purpose of displaying some of the difficulties with which university administrations are confronted in dealing with certain types of professors."

It seems clear that Elliott was not prepared to assume that the complaining faculty members were invariably correct in their claims and the administrators invariably wrong. Moreover, it is also apparent that he was not willing to help create a pressure group which spoke only and always for the faculty without investigating the justice of the claim.

Along with other cases being actively investigated by the group during the summer of 1915, plans were made to investigate the case of the three professors at Montana. A sub-committee was appointed by Seligman with C. A. Kofoid, University of California, as chairman; Elliott, along with others, was named a member of the Montana committee. Shortly after Kofoid wrote to Elliott giving a brief outline of the plan for investigating the Montana case, Elliott was compelled to reply, "The situation is indeed paradoxical. Last Tuesday I accepted the chancellorship of the higher educational institutions of the state of Montana . . . ." Elliott explained that he assumed that he was no longer eligible to serve as a member, but that he greatly regretted the necessity of "severing connections with the very important movement represented by the Committee of 15."

In a similar letter to Lovejoy, who had been elected secretary of the AAUP, he wrote that although he was not sure of the proper procedure to follow, he felt that he should withdraw from the Committee on Academic Freedom because he was probably ineligible to be a member of the AAUP. "While I do not assume the office until February 1, 1916," he wrote, "it seems appropriate that my withdrawal should take place now . . . ." He told Lovejoy that he believed that he could make a contribution to the cause of academic freedom, however, as chancellor of the University of Montana. He was dropped immediately from the membership.

It seems certain that Elliott was the first man to lose his charter membership in the Association—his tenure lasted just eight and one-half months! In the weeks and months that followed, however, the chancellor was kept in frequent contact with his friends on the Committee of Fifteen and was listed as an honorary member of the organization.

THE AAUP INVESTIGATION

Once the machinery had been set in motion for an investigation of the dismissal of the three professors in Montana, the Committee of Fifteen felt obliged to complete its report. As a result of pressure from the AAUP as well as from other groups, the Montana State Board of Education voted in October to reinstate the three professors, but gave them a leave of absence for one year and reportedly agreed that the time and condition of their return to active service would rest with the chancellor.

Elliott was elected chancellor at this same meeting (October 11, 1915), but, according to his later statement, "not until several weeks after, . . . did I receive any information relative to the reinstatement and the above understanding."

He wrote to Lovejoy on October 22 to present his view of the dismissals:

"During my preliminary negotiations regarding the chancellorship, the most disturbing factor was the summary dismissal of the three professors last June. In my first conference with members of the State Board of Education, after listening to all of the evidence given me, I said that in my judgment the June action of the board violated every essential principle of sound educational administration and at the same time lacked the ordinary requirement of equity. In stating this conclusion, of course, I had no particular reference to the merit or demerits of any particular case. The procedure of the Board represents the issue at stake."

By the middle of November, Lovejoy felt that he understood all aspects of the case and assured Elliott that "the feeling of professors Seligman, Dewey, and myself, at least, is that the paramount consideration for our committee is that of avoiding, for the present, a further stirring up of . . . antagonism so that your administration may not in any way be handicapped by anything that we do."

Elliott, meanwhile, had learned that the board expected him to see that the professors were *not* placed on active duty when their leave expired. At a meeting of the State Board of Education on December 6, he made it perfectly clear to the members of the board that, in view of the character of the controversy, he would not assume any responsibility for the future status of the three professors. Elliott wrote later that in his judgment, "the Board had, as to its procedure in dismissing these persons, committed a grave error; that this error was greatly intensified by the reinstatement; and that the responsibility for any final decision on these cases must be assumed directly and exclusively by the Board."

During December 1915, two of the dismissed professors came to see Elliott at Madison. When he wrote of this to Governor Stewart, Elliott said that the question of their future relationships to the university was one that would have to be settled by the board of education.

The governor's reply left no doubt as to the final disposition of the case. "The Board reinstated them to clear up their professional reputation, as that was the one thing that was harped upon all along the line. If as a matter of fact," he said, "they were deceiving us and wanted to hold their jobs, then, of course, there is nothing left but the knife . . . ." Stewart, however, later was quite obviously attempting to shift the responsibility from the board to the chancellor; but Elliott was determined not to become involved. He reasoned that since the action had taken place before he had been employed, the board, and not the chancellor, was responsible for the disposition of the case.

Lovejoy soon sensed what was going on and wrote to Elliott in January saying that the committee would be highly disturbed to see "a situation in which the Board escapes responsibility in this matter by referring it to the chancellor and the chancellor similiarly escapes responsibility by referring it to the Board." He concluded, "I hope, however, when you actually assume office, you will be able to straighten things out. They assuredly sadly need straightening."

Elliott, obviously nettled by this letter which came while he was still at Madison attempting to complete the hundreds of details connected with his leaving, dictated a short reply: "May I request," he wrote, "that any judgment upon the matter referred to in your letter of January 17, be suspended until there is an opportunity for me to assume an official attitude or to take official action. This I have not yet done. Neither will I do so until I am actually in office."

Not to be deterred, Professor Lovejoy replied patiently, "I am glad to have your note . . . . We shall, of course, be glad to wait until you have had an opportunity to take official action in the matter."

The exchange of correspondence with Lovejoy continued during the next few months. Elliott maintained his position, but explained that one of the conditions of his acceptance of the chancellorship was "that the Board of Education should provide definite tenure for the members of the   faculty . . . other   than   that provided by the former system of annual elections." "Details of this plan are now in the process of development, in cooperation with the president and faculties of the different institutions," he wrote. "As soon as this plan is completed I shall be glad to inform you."

Finally, in September 1916, Elliott wrote to Lovejoy suggesting that the committee report, if published, would not contribute to the solution of any difficulty, but, on the contrary, might serve to reopen old controversies.

A week later Elliott wrote again to Lovejoy suggesting that the committee undertake "to state the reverse of the issue: that is, not only the obligation which the institution has toward its staff but also the obligation which the members of the staff have toward the institution." He went ahead to relate an experience in which a full professor, whose salary had been increased substantially above the maximum and with whom there was a "gentlemen's agreement" relative to his return, announced his resignation two weeks before the university session opened. "If the committee has not yet undertaken to define the limits of individual responsibility," he observed, "would it not be appropriate to do this?"

The final result was that in May 1917 the committee report was published in a bulletin of the association. The report reviewed the essentials of the dispute, not mentioning that Elliott had been a member of the committee, and concluded:

> The committee fully recognizes that Dr. Elliott found himself in a difficult, delicate, and embarrassing situation, not of his own creation, from which there was no wholly satisfactory way out. It seems to the committee, nevertheless, that, by accepting the chancellorship, Dr. Elliott obligated himself—as a simple matter of good faith on the part of the institution whose executive he thereby became —to make good the promises given in behalf of the Board by its chairman to the dismissed professors and to this committee.

The report continued,

> The committee is unable to distinguish so nicely as does Chancellor Elliott between his official and personal acts, and is constrained to recognize that, while professing to have nothing to do with the cases of the three professors, he actually did throw his influence against their reinstatement. According to his own testimony, he expressed to the Board the view that their action in reinstating the dismissed professors was in error—an attitude which must greatly have weighed with them, and may well have been the decisive factor in determining them to reverse that action. It seems equally clear to the committee that if he had favored such a course, either genuine reinstatement, or genuine hearings, would have been assured.

> The committee is reluctantly forced to announce that, despite the assurances received from time to time that progress was being made, no regulations governing for the future the appointments, dismissals, and tenure of office of the faculty of the University of Montana have yet been adopted.

The report was scarcely noticed in Montana in 1917, however, as time had nearly obscured the early controversies. As it turned out, in 1918 a plan was adopted which provided adequate guarantees of tenure and seemed to please both the faculty and administration.

The fact that the AAUP was a new organization, eager to prove its worth to the profession, certainly accounts to a large degree for the aggressive nature of its report. Lovejoy, in particular, was fired with righteous indignation, and the very nature of his position prevented him from viewing the situation as it might be interpreted in later years. While Elliott might have influenced the board to retain the three professors, there is considerable evidence to the contrary. In view of the fact that Elliott had staked his reputation on the premise that he would bring about a wholesome development among the higher schools of the state, he could hardly have been expected to start his career under the shadow of a particular faction. He strongly felt that his first obligation was to the people of the state, and an honest trial of the new administration demanded a fresh start for all concerned. He was pioneering in an uncharted area, and to him the matter of prime importance was that of setting up an efficient organization of higher institutions. All other considerations, even the fate of three professors, were secondary.

THE INAUGURAL YEAR

The people of Montana, of course, were hardly aware of the AAUP investigation even at its peak in January 1916. The newspapers of the state late in 1915 were largely concerned with the chancellor as a person; and the news stories indicated that Elliott had favorably impressed many people in the state with his personal magnetism.

During the first two months in office he attended numerous banquets given in his honor but managed to maintain his "vow of silence" concerning university policies. Several editorials noted that Elliott had made a wise stipulation when he insisted that he not be asked to deliver public addresses for at least six months after assuming his new duties.

His first official request was calculated to catch the public eye when he asked that the American flag be flown over the campus at Missoula every day that the weather permitted. A few days later it was made known that he had declined an invitation to take part in a survey of the state of Washington—the reason: "Too much work to do in Montana."

By the middle of February 1916, the *Butte Miner* declared, "Dr. Elliott certainly has made a splendid start," and the *Daily Missoulian* announced, "All that has drifted in and out is convincing that the governor and the state board have been fortunate in the selection of Dr. Elliott to guide out of chaos the collegiate institutions of this state." After hearing Elliott give one of his informal talks one reporter wrote, "Chancellor Elliott has a voluminous vocabulary, which when combined with his brilliant mind and strong and pleasing voice, makes him an entertaining speaker . . . ." Even papers which were violently opposed to Governor Stewart, such as *The New Northwest,* owned by former president Craighead, were praising Elliott.

Late in March 1916, he sent a letter to every school principal and superintendent asking for their cooperation. "I am of the firm belief," he wrote, "that any permanent success of the new plan is to a very large degree dependent upon the counsel, the friendly criticism and the constant cooperation of the men and women directing the work of the public elementary and high schools." He asked that the school administrators complete a brief questionnaire which might provide him with some advice and suggestions for improving the relationships between the various institutions of the university and the other parts of the public school system. It was a step clearly designed to establish a good working relationship between the university administration and the public school administrators of the state; a gratifying response may have helped him shape future policies.

An announcement in May 1916 told of an innovation designed to bring about more efficient operation. According to a newspaper report, each of the four state institutions had in former years sent representatives to visit the high schools of the state in an effort to gain students; these representatives generally had set forth only the advantages offered by their particular institution. Under the new plan the state was to be divided into districts and only one insitution was to send a representative into a particular area. The chancellor advised and instructed each high school visitor to remember, "You are serving as a representative, not of your particular institution, but of all of the institutions of the University." Similarly, Elliott announced that where four posters had appeared extolling the advantages of each of the schools, in the future a single poster would be prepared which would give identical publicity to each of the four institutions.

In addition to implementing these kinds of ideas, Elliott immediately set out to meet with as many groups as he could. He spent weeks organizing a strong alumni association which joined the four smaller, separate organizations into a federated Montana Alumni Club. He arranged for an *Alumni Quarterly* to be published by the chancellor's office which gave him a direct contact with a group of citizens most certainly interested in the progress of the university.

One of the first internal projects concerned a new plan of budget control. Previous sessions of the legislature had been plagued by lobbyists from each of the four schools, and many legislators had favored the chancellor plan simply because it promised relief from the insistent and unorganized demands for appropriations. Under the new plan the chancellor's office was to prepare a combined budget for consideration by the legislature.

In another budget-related move, Elliott secured the services of an accountant for the purpose of establishing a uniform system of accounting for the several higher institutions. Within four months he announced that a budget plan for financial control had been introduced. "Each budget first sets forth the source from which the money comes," he said, "the amount available, and in general the departments in which it will be expended. Then follow in detail the specified uses in each department of the institution which the allotted expenditure will cover . . . ."

At the same time he brought the director of dormitories at the University of Chicago to Montana to study the dormitory system for a few weeks in an effort to improve efficiency and reduce costs.

From February until June he was able to give virtually all his attention to the job at hand, for his family was still in Madison. Mrs. Elliott stayed behind with their four small children, declining to make the trip West until late spring; for John, the oldest son, was seven years old, and the baby, Edward, Jr., was just a year old. When the worst of the weather was past, they moved to the first of three rented homes in Helena. The third one, where they lived for the longest period, was a large residence at 428 Power Street. It was a lovely home on a sizeable lot and the family was delighted with the style of living in Montana.

The series of ceremonies marking the inauguration of the chancellor began at Dillon, May 30, 1916, at a banquet at the college; the following day inaugural ceremonies were held in connection with commencement exercises. On June 1, the party made up of the four presidents, the state board, and the chancellor visited the School of Mines at Butte where his inaugural address was again delivered. Two days later the group visited the college at Bozeman and the inaugural address was given following the commencement exercise. Ceremonies were concluded at Missoula on June 8, at the commencement exercises of the State University. Once again the visiting presidents conveyed the greetings of the other state institutions and the formal addresses were delivered.

Elliott's inaugural address was a clear, concise statement of policy, and is one of the best accounts of the basic understandings developed and accepted by him during his career in higher education. It contained a number of paragraphs that he had prepared for his address at the University of Idaho in 1910.

Reviewing the aims of the modern state university, Elliott noted that the university was generally accepted as the means of transmitting human culture from one generation to another, training civic leaders and professional experts, and extending the boundaries of knowledge and truth. But at that time, he continued, a fourth aim, commonly called "service to the state," was coming to be generally accepted. This "service" aim required that all of the people of the state receive "daily dividends from that knowledge, ability, and opportunity which they have capitalized in these institutions."

He suggested that a new field of service to the people of the state might be found in the area of retail buying and selling. A second area in which the university might perform a service was that of politics. "The University of that state that does not undertake a scientific study of political problems today is out of the current of life," he advised.

Reviewing the new university administrative plan he noted that "there is not to be found in any American state a scheme of organization and government similar to that devised by the legislature of 1913 for the University of Montana." It was clearly an educational experiment, he observed, but he believed that it might solve many of Montana's perplexing problems and would "undoubtedly influence the higher educational organizations of more than a score of American states in which the same problems are to be found."

Among several other items which he briefly discussed, two were of particular interest not only within the state, but in other states as well. He proposed, first, that the state assume the actual cost of travel (less $5.00) for every capable student for one round-trip each year from his home community to any one of the institutions of the university. The cost would be insignificant he said, when compared with the advantages of having the institution "near the door" of every home in the state and the plan would give "a new significance to the doctrine that a higher and professional education is open equally to the sons and daughters of the state." The legislature, evidently pleased with the novel idea, authorized the State Board of Education in 1917 to provide each student with a travel refund as outlined by Elliott.

The second item which received considerable attention over the nation and was later reprinted by Edgar W. Knight in *What College Presidents Say* referred to the matter of state financial support.[1] Elliott suggested that a lesson could be drawn from the fact that "it now costs the taxpayers of the state two dollars for the care of the unfortunates in the state penitentiary and the state asylum as compared to one dollar for the education of the students in the university colleges and schools."

Concluding his address, Elliott spelled out his convictions in unmistakable terms:

> As chancellor of the University, I will not consider that I have served the full purpose of my office until the vast majority of the people of Montana of whatever class or occupation come to feel freely that their University is a worthy agency, ever at their disposal, for aiding them to meet the needs that determine the happiness, the satisfactions and the ideals of their lives; until there is firmly established among students and teachers the principle that work makes education possible, education must in turn make work possible.

It was this statement, with only minor changes, which he later used as his "personal charter" when he became president of Purdue University and still later was widely circulated as Elliott's "Purdue Philosophy." (The last time he publicly expressed this same idea was thirty-nine years later (in July 1955) when the eighty-year-old Elliott spoke at the University of Nebraska on the occasion of the sixtieth anniversary of his graduation.)

It was late summer before Elliott elected to make his second major public address. The occasion was a meeting of the Montana State Banker's Association, and he used it to good advantage.

Elliott related that when he came to the state of Montana he soon realized that he had four things to do: establish amicable and harmonious relationships between the four higher schools; coordinate the work of these institutions so that duplication of efforts could be eliminated; effect a greater economy in the money being expended by these four schools; and, finally, accept the responsibility of keeping the citizenship of the state fully and accurately informed regarding the work of the institution.

But as he concluded his talk, still another matter of no small importance to Elliott was presented to the group. He asked that the association establish a loan fund of $1,000 and place it at the disposal of university authorities for the purpose of assisting worthy students. "If there is one thing our institutions need now," he said, "it is a little ready money that we can loan to a student at a very low or at no interest at all and he may pay back when he gets out into the earning world . . . ."

The association gave $1,000 to establish a student loan fund which was later increased until in July 1917 a total of $5,000 was set aside for student use.

In October 1916, an editorial in the *Helena Independent* observed:

> We wonder if Montana has ever witnessed more effective work than that of Chancellor Elliott? In a comparatively short period he has restored peace in the University and is building up the affiliated schools into a powerful body. It requires no stretch of the imagination to see Montana's University, within a decade, one of the largest of the land, in point of attendance.
> Taking the schools out of politics was the only solution for the ills that attend them; and the chancellor system was the only feasible way to do it. But even while the method itself is admirable, far less might have been accomplished had not Montana been so fortunate as to secure Dr. Elliott. His quiet, effective methods stamped him one of the great educators—and executives —now living.

Even before the year had closed, the office of the chancellor was functioning effectively and Elliott was free to accept invitations to address the Colorado State Teachers Association in Denver, a meeting of presidents of state universities in Washington, D.C., the Montana State Teachers Association in Missoula, and the Wyoming State Teachers Association in Laramie.

THE WAR YEARS

The first few months in 1917 were as busy as any of the months in the preceding year. The legislature was in session and Elliott was having his first direct contact with legislative budget control.

Yet at the same time, with the nation concerned over the war in Europe, a number of conferences were held with the board and various administrative heads relating to university war-time policy. Elliott and the others talked mostly of practicing economy until the issues in the international crisis were defined. Echoing General Leonard Wood, the chancellor said to the students, "Stay on your present job until you are called." And after a meeting in Washington, D.C., in May 1917, he reiterated, "The best service can be rendered by educating and equipping yourselves for a work that only educated persons can perform."

The total university enrollment was up 20 to 30 per cent in Setpember 1917, and Elliott promptly outlined the need for new buildings. But with war clouds hanging over state and nation, there was little consideration given his requests for increased appropriations. The citizens were more concerned over the fact that athletic events had been cancelled (May 5, 1917) and that the German language was still being taught in the schools. As the school year was drawing to a close in April 1918, the chancellor felt obliged to comment for the papers, ". . . it is even more important now for us to have a knowledge of German language than it was before the war. We are not adding to our fighting strength by keeping ourselves in ignorance of the enemy."

The Students' Army Training Corps was organized in Washington, D.C., in July 1918, and Elliott was appointed one of eleven divisional directors. He was in charge of the division which included the states of Montana, Washington, Oregon, Idaho, and Wyoming. His schedule for the next few months remained hectic as he travelled to Washington for numerous meetings and made many trips throughout the five state area. The war ended before the organizational work was completed, but in December 1918, Elliott was commended by Director R. C. MacLaurin (president of Massachusetts Institute of Technology) for his work.

For his services as regional director, Elliott was paid the sum of $800. Rather than keep the money, he established a loan fund in March 1920 to be known as the Nebraska Alumni Loan Fund, which the State Board of Education later renamed the Elliott Loan Fund.

Early in 1919, there was some concerted effort in the legislature to abolish the post of chancellor of the University of Montana. The old argument was repeated which called attention to the expense of maintaining the office of the chancellor. The chancellor's salary (then at $10,000 per year) was discussed at great length for there was some opposition in the legislature to the salary figure since the Governor's salary was somewhat lower; but no action was taken. Elliott still had strong support in the capital from the people of the state.

THE LEVINE CASE

In February 1919, a second incident involving the dismissal of a professor occurred which provoked new controversy, gained the attention of Eastern newspapers, called forth critical comments from several liberal writers, and yet seemingly had little lasting effect on Elliott's popularity in the state.

A year earlier Elliott and President E. O. Sisson of the State University at Missoula had worked out a plan to issue a series of six bulletins on taxation in Montana; one was scheduled as *The Taxation of Mines In Montana* to be prepared by Dr. Louis Levine. Levine had come to State University in 1916 as an instructor with the understanding that he would have an opportunity to do research work on the tax bulletin, and he was promised financial assistance in the preparation of his work.

In November 1918, when Elliott reviewed the nearly completed bulletin, he suggested to Levine that it might not be advisable to publish it as a university document since the bulletin clearly involved matters of political moment.

It contained statements which accused the mines, particularly the Anaconda Copper Mining Company, of not paying their proper share of taxes, largely as a result of alleged inequitable assessments. The matter of assessments had long been the subject of political controversy, and just at that period the university was also being accused of teaching socialism, county agents were allegedly soliciting membership for the Non-Partisan League, and the university was generally under light fire in newspapers scattered over the state.

The chancellor decided that the university should not sponsor the paper because he felt obligated to protect the institution from further criticism which might affect the conduct of the university affairs. President Sisson concurred, but both agreed that Levine was free to publish it at his own expense.

At a second meeting in December 1918, the chancellor reiterated his decision, so Levine acquiesced and placed the papers in the hand of a private publisher.

The following month, however, when Governor Stewart found time to read a copy of the paper which Elliott had submitted to him several weeks earlier, he immediately called in the chancellor to advise him that the bulletin should not be published. It ". . . would raise up powerful enemies against the university," he declared.

So Elliott again attempted to dissuade Levine although apparently he did not *order* Levine to stop publication. President Sisson felt that Levine could publish at his own expense and took no part in urging Levine to halt his plan.

When the publication appeared in print, Governor Stewart left it to the chancellor to determine what action should be taken. Elliott later told the board as he reviewed the case, "I tried to make him (Levine) understand that the University came first and that I regarded it my duty to look out for the college under the circumstances." "Dr. Levine saw fit not to observe my advice in the matter and he published the monograph on mine taxation. I therefore suspended him for insubordination, for conduct unbecoming a member of the faculty, basing my action on the rules of the State Board of Education."

When Levine's suspension was announced on February 7, 1919, a sizeable portion of the faculty was aroused and notified the AAUP, taking the view that the suspension represented a serious breach of academic freedom. As a result of this action the case became rather widely publicized. Various liberal newspapers described the case as an example of the complete dominance which the mining interests, notably the Anaconda Copper Mining Company, maintained over the state of Montana.

Elliott, however, had set up the Faculty Service Committee the previous year to review any administrative decision which seemed to the faculty to be unwise or in any way unfair. This committee, composed by one member chosen by the chancellor, one by the faculty, and one by the professor involved, was quietly called to review the circumstances of the suspension. In their report they asked that the State Board of Education hold a hearing; and a hearing was convened in April in order that the facts of the case could be presented.

The final solution, reached after the hearing, was a disturbing one to many people. The board upheld Elliott's actions, but then reinstated Levine and paid him for the time he was under suspension; they voted approval of Elliott's action six to three, then voted for Levine's reinstatement by the same margin. In addition the board passed an amendment which served as an admonition to the chancellor and quieted faculty objections. They changed the rule which gave the chancellor the authority to suspend a faculty member so that it would read "until investigation by a regular or special meeting of the board." Later newspaper accounts were discouraging.

Practically every paper displayed concern over the obvious attempt of the board to smother Levine's report. To the editors it was a sign that politicians were back in the schools and that the university was a "public shuttlecock." To faculty members it was a question of free speech and, while it had taken a struggle, Levine had been vindicated in their eyes. To the members of the alumni association it was an opportunity to make an effort to secure representation on the State Board of Education.

To Upton Sinclair, who reported the incident in *The Goose Step*,[2] it was further "proof" of his thesis that "our educational system is not a public service, but an instrument of special privilege; its purpose is not to further the welfare of mankind, but merely to keep America capitalistic." The Sinclair account unfortunately was written with an evident bias and contained a few totally incorrect statements. Other contrived statements made implications not based on facts, although he certainly made a vivid presentation of the case.

To the citizens of the state it was a regrettable situation and no doubt many people were puzzled at the reports of the affair. The public accounts could not help but take away some of the lustre which had surrounded the chancellor and the chancellorship plan. "Better for Dr. Elliott to have been a hero and a martyr than a politican, taking care to protect the money side of the college," wrote an anonymous contributor to the "Letters" column of the *Helena Record-Herald*. But the following month a joint committee of the legislature investigating the greater university had nothing but high praise for the system and its chancellor.

A summary record of the case was published in the AAUP Bulletin in May 1919, which carefully pointed out that Elliott's Administrative Memo No. 100, adopted on June 22, 1918, had set up the Faculty Service Committee "for the purpose of securing to all administrative officers and members of instructional staffs proper professional tenure . . . ." The association report concluded that the case had been "closed satisfactorily through the reinstatement of Professor Levine."

While an account of the incident can never hope to convince an extremist that the chancellor was absolutely justified, a satisfactory explanation does appear possible. Elliott acted to preserve the growing strength of the university. He felt that his primary obligation to the board and to the people was to maintain a strong university, and to accomplish this he needed appropriations from the legislature.

Only a few people in the state knew better than the chancellor the power which the mining companies directed. He also knew that the report prepared by Levine was essentially correct; but the paper was prepared as an *attack* on the mines rather than an unbiased report; and most important, it was the wrong time, because of the forthcoming legislative session, to release the report.

It would be ridiculous to suppose that the chancellor did not realize what a storm of criticism would be raised over the suspension notice. He could be confident, however, that his action in setting up the Faculty Service Committee would absolve him of the charge of dictatorship. And what was of greater importance to him, at the moment—he could be reasonably sure that the budgets would pass the legislature.

Elliott's decision to dismiss Levine was a realistically calculated move. As a result, the budget was passed; Levine was reinstated, proving the wisdom of the system of checks and balances within the faculty; and the chancellor's policy of insisting that university staff members should not mix in legislative political controversy was made clear.

It would appear that Elliott's earlier move to develop a university code, a fairly elaborate set of policies, rules and regulations, together with a committee structure to handle faculty matters, made it possible for the Levine case to be resolved without destroying the effectiveness of the chancellorship.

THE UNIVERSITY CODE

Soon after Elliott had arrived in Helena he began discussing plans to publish a university code, but the preparatory work was tedious and time consuming, so that the first part of the code was not published until June 1919. Part I of the University of Montana Code contained federal statutes, rulings, regulations, and instructions; state constitutional provisions; and state statutes which regulated the administration of the state schools.

Part II of the code was made available in 1918, but only in loose-leaf, mimeographed form. This second part contained regulations for the internal administration of the schools. It included the aims of the university, the duties of the chancellor, the general scheme of organization of the university, and regulations concerning the staff of the university. Since many of these regulations were in the trial stage, still under careful consideration, Part II did not appear in print until after Elliott had left Montana for his post at Purdue University.

FINANCIAL PROBLEMS

One of the most serious problems confronting the chancellor during the early years in Montana was simply the matter of getting sufficient funds to operate the greater university. The first step toward the solution was that of setting up a budget system; the next was that of publishing an annual report for the people of the state. The chancellor wanted a financial report that could be readily understood by the citizens who were expected to provide the money necessary to perpetuate the higher schools. It was part of his program to build up confidence in state schools in the minds of the people of the state.

When the first financial report was published in November 1918, covering the fiscal year 1917-1918, it was, as far as Elliott could determine, the first time that a financial report of the university institutions had been published.

Two additional annual reports were published in 1919 and 1920, then in 1921 it was decided to substitute a biennial report plan, the first issue to be compiled in 1922. A section of each report was devoted to general explanations and comments not necessarily related to finances which gave the chancellor an opportunity to report on what had been accomplished within the university and to make recommendations for future action.

The reports indicated that the most immediate problems, according to Elliott, were related to finances: the state had no well-defined policy which would guarantee dollars to meet increasing needs for both day-to-day operations and for the construction of buildings. The establishing of a centralized accounting system and a central purchasing department were important steps toward better financial control under the budget system, but Elliott wanted larger and more secure financial support.

No new buildings had been constructed at the university, for example, during the ten years prior to the time Elliott took office. Practically all facilities were overcrowded, and plans for the expansion of the physical plant had to be made before plans for an increased enrollment could be furthered.

The board authorized Elliott to employ Cass Gilbert, a consulting architect from New York City, to work out plans for campus development. During the next few years, largely as a result of this planning, land was gradually acquired by the separate institutions. By June 1919, university officials were able to present a proposed plan for campus development at both Missoula and Bozeman.

Even with the limited funds available three new buildings were completed in 1919; a natural science laboratory at State University, a women's dormitory at State Normal College, and a chemistry laboratory at State College to replace a building destroyed by fire in 1916.

The heart of the financial problem which prevented any considerable expansion originated in the state constitution which placed a limit of two and one half mills as a maximum levy for general taxation for all state purposes. The value of taxable property in the state was increasing, but another constitutional provision reduced the rate of state taxation by twenty per cent as soon as the total assessed valuation reached six hundred million dollars. It was estimated that the assessed valuation would reach that figure in 1920.

The state government appropriations had exceeded revenues for twenty years. Deficiencies had accumulated until the state was virtually a year behind in its finances, and the amount of money available for the university was very closely restricted. Since the university depended on state appropriations for more than sixty per cent of the total amounts necessary to maintain operations, the situation was intolerable. There was hardly enough money appropriated for current expenses, and none left for an ambitious building program. Thus, the time had come to attempt a wide-spread change.

THE UNIVERSITY FUNDS CAMPAIGN

During the summer of 1919, the chancellor, working with the presidents of the four state schools and certain other of his friends in the legislature, developed a plan which would provide for a state tax of one and one half mills to be levied for a period of ten years and appropriated largely for university purposes; a second measure would authorize the issuance of bonds to the amount of five million dollars for the construction of necessary buildings. The chancellor presented these plans to the State Board of Education at its December meeting in 1919 and secured the board's endorsement. The approval was a qualified one, however, for the legality of such a bond issue had not been established in Montana.

The chancellor's recommendation was that these two measures be referred to the people of the state at the next general election. Although the state constitution provided for initiative and referendum, the voters could not demand an appropriation of funds. Because the bond issue was not an appropriation, the board was willing to provide a test case.

In order to get the two measures on the ballot for the November 1920 election, the signatures of approximately twenty thousand registered voters, distributed over various parts of the state, had to be secured. For this primary purpose the University Funds Campaign was launched by the chancellor and the board. Various board members and others donated a total of twenty-five thousand dollars to support the drive to secure ultimate approval of the two measures.

While the campaign was organized initially to get the necessary signatures, a second part of the task was to get the matter out in the open, squarely before all the voters in the state. "The University of Montana belongs to the people of the state. If they do not want it to go forward and are not willing to meet the expense of putting it forward, it is for them to say," Elliott wrote. "But to acquaint them with the actual situation . . . is no small job."

The general supervision of the University Funds Campaign was under the direction of Elliott and the four school presidents, but Professor W. F. Brewer of State College was in direct charge. The state was divided into sixteen districts and by March 1920 the district chairmen (all college professors) had been organized to lead the campaign.

The chancellor initiated the campaign at Charter Day exercises in Missoula on February 17, 1920. During the next few months he made dozens of talks to groups over the state. By June 25, enough signatures had been obtained to insure that the measures would be on the ballot at the general election in November.

Six thousand copies of a *Workers' Handbook* containing information about the university and its needs were printed and distributed during the summer. Posters and placards appeared in every community and university representatives spoke before every important meeting. Both political parties endorsed the measures, and even the ministers of the state were asked to devote the services of October 17 to a discussion of the critical needs of the university.

At the November election the voters favored the initiative measures by a decisive note. The mill tax passed 82,669 to 71,169 while the bond issue passed 90,441 to 66,237.

One of the editors of the *Educational Review* wrote of the campaign:

> Notwithstanding the diversions of a heated political campaign, the depression following the war, and three years of disastrous drought, the campaign of education for education was victorious. The people

of Montana have translated their civic ideals into terms that cannot
be misunderstood . . . .

Almost immediately the building program began to unfold.
Bonds totalling seven hundred thousand dollars were offered for
sale and when school opened in 1921, Elliott announced that work
was under way on thirteen new buildings. The total cost was estimated at $1,875,000. Included in this ambitious program was a
new library, a forestry building, new residence halls, new buildings for the heating plants, new engineering buildings, a new din-
ing hall and kitchen, a metallurgical building, and two new
gymnasia.

In January 1922, however, the chancellor announced that no
further sale of bonds would be made even though almost one
third of the maximum dollars available remained to be issued in
bonds. There was considerable dissatisfaction with the weight of
the tax increase, and the State Board of Education thought it
inadvisable to increase the interest burden. The tremendous task
had been accomplished, however, and the university was on a
firm financial basis.

When the results of the University Funds Campaign were reviewed by those responsible for higher education in other states,
the Montana plan for university administration was probably re-
examined with new interest. The experiment "attracted wide attention among practical administrators throughout the country,"
reported one writer, who also announced that "a legislative commission from the state of California visited the Montana institution for the purpose of observing first-hand the workings of the
organization, and reporting to the California legislature, in hope
of gaining valuable light on the problems of that state."

It is also likely that the members of the Board of Trustees of
Purdue University were interested in such reports, for the university was operating under the temporary administrative leadership
of the vice president of the board.

While the negotiations between Elliott and the officials at Purdue University are detailed in the next chapter, it is a matter
of record that on May 12, 1922, Elliott submitted his letter of
resignation to Montana's governor and thus closed out his career
as chancellor of the University of Montana.

In his letter of resignation Elliott pointed out that he had declined several offers of other positions in recent years, any one

of which "promised opportunities for the kind of distinctly educational service in which I am primarily interested. However, I considered myself obligated," he continued, "to see certain important projects, essential to the future welfare of the university organizations, brought to a substantial completion. Now I feel that I have done my share of the pioneering task and may retire with no sense of remissness."

Elliott was tired. Although the chancellor's office was in the Capitol Building in Helena, he had visited each campus for a few days at least once each month and usually could count on only weekends at home. For more than five years he had had little time to write and had published only about one-fourth as many articles as he had published during the preceding five year period. There had been little time for the chancellor to engage in any outside activities, and he had told a friend that he keenly felt "the disadvantages of the geographic isolation."

One activity which he refused to drop, however, was the so-called Cleveland Conference, which served especially well to help keep the chancellor in touch with educational affairs over the country and enabled him to visit more or less regularly with good friends on an informal basis.

THE CLEVELAND CONFERENCE

The Cleveland Conference, as it came to be known, started in January 1915, when Elliott and Judd met with Leonard Ayres of the Russell Sage Foundation and Walter Jessup of the University of Iowa, for a couple of days in a hotel in Cleveland to talk about the Cleveland survey (conducted by the Russell Sage Foundation) which was nearing completion; but the discussion soon led to a more or less general session on topics in education of mutual interest.

Judd was particularly enthused and thought that the four should meet at least annually and invite other leaders in education to join the informal session. So in January 1916, another group session was held in Cleveland with eleven participants. Judd had written to sixteen other leaders besides the original four, but Walter Jessup, James R. Angell, Abraham Flexner, Paul Hanus, Charles N. Kendall, Bruce Payne, David Snedden, Frank E. Spaulding, and E. L. Thorndike could not attend. The eleven who did meet in 1916 were Judd, Ayres, Elliott, D. C. Bliss, Charles E.

Chadsey, Lotus Coffman, Ellwood Cubberley, Paul Monroe, E. C. Moore, Henry C. Morrison, and George Strayer. Over half of the group were Teachers College men.

The Cleveland Conference was based on purely personal relationships, completely informal, and because of the wide range of interests represented, the members got "the intimate context of what . . . (was) . . . happening in the educational world." Elliott attended every year from 1915 to 1926 and, after a lapse of eight years, rejoined the group for an additional three years.

These meetings were of tremendous value in keeping the chancellor in close contact with others in the profession, and they never failed to provide a pleasant and stimulating break from the more formal contacts dictated by his position. Elliott thought that perhaps it was his association with this group that led President Lowell to ask him to join the staff at Harvard in 1920. Elliott laughed when he recalled that although he had always discussed with his wife the various offers extended to him, he declined this appointment without telling Mrs. Elliott until the deed was done.

The reason was simple. Elliott at that time was completely wrapped up in the fund campaign that promised to give the Montana institutions enough money for a huge building program. Even though the Harvard position was attractive, he could not bring himself to leave Montana while in sight of victory. Knowing that Mrs. Elliott had had the considerable task of managing the home and four growing children, he reasoned that she would have welcomed the quiet and relatively settled life at Cambridge; so he spared her the regret by failing to mention the offer until the decision had been made. As it turned out, he said, she was not at all anxious to go East, anyway.

The Purdue offer came, however, at a time when he could hardly resist the temptation to leave. "While I have a certain satisfaction in the constructive results which have been accomplished in the development and unification of the University of Montana during the past six years and more," he told the governor, "I cannot longer remain unmindful of the constant heavy drain upon my strength and endurance, especially on account of the multitude of exacting details . . . ." Continuing, he expressed the thought that Mrs. Elliott was eager to hear. "Most of all," he wrote, "do I regret the official demands which have kept me away from my home and my family the major part of the time of my residence in Montana."

The newspapers of the state, of course, carried a number of stories concerning his resignation. An editorial in *The Daily Missoulian* stated:

> Dr. Elliott is a rare combination of the business executive and the highly trained educator. He is gifted with grasp and decision, great capacity for work and unswerving loyalty to his job. Under his administration there has been great progress in all departments . . . . Especially is this true of State University, and we regard his departure as most unfortunate . . . . Dr. Elliott is in the very prime of vigorous manhood with the best part of his career ahead.

Other papers over the state had even warmer praise for the chancellor and his work. An article in the *Alumni Quarterly* which set out to review Elliott's work in Montana listed some of the accomplishments of the past six years but concluded that perhaps the most important achievement was the developing of the habit of unity and cooperation among the constituent institutions.

In his final letter to the alumni, however, Elliott wrote, "The outstanding, permanent feature of the development of the past six years is, in my judgment, to be found in the fact that the co-ordinated university has been given an enduring place in the civic consciousness of the people of the state."

Ten years later Elliott's successor, M. A. Brannon, who was perhaps in a better position to evaluate Elliott's work in Montana than was any other educator, wrote:

> In place of four separate, competing institutions, operating without budgets, employing different methods of accounting, encroaching wherever possible upon the work of one another, and each feeling more or less that it possessed vested rights, Dr. Elliott left a coordinated university composed of four units, with business offices thoroughly modernized and operating with budgets; with vital, experimental and enterprising faculties; with duplication of courses minimized and eliminated and with a consuming desire to give higher educational service to students and to improve steadily in all public service relations.

Noting that Elliott had no precedents to study or follow, he nevertheless "built exceedingly well and displayed unusual foresight and wisdom in elaborating the details and techniques of an enlarged and coordinated institution," Brannon wrote in 1932.[3]

Then in 1966, fifty years after Elliott's inauguration, the university took action to honor him in another way; a married student housing complex was named "Elliott Village." The project, which contained 174 units constructed at a cost of $1,600,000, was opened in Missoula by University of Montana President Robert Johns; it will undoubtedly remain as a permanent memorial to the first chancellor.

During his tenure at Montana, Elliott had survived some troubled times with the faculty, had gained confidence in his ability to deal with board members and legislators, and had learned that he was happiest doing administrative work in higher education. Half-way through his career, he was to spend the next twenty-three years at Purdue University doing the things he enjoyed most.

NOTES

1. Edgar W. Knight, *What College Presidents Say* (Chapel Hill: The University of North Carolina Press, 1940), pp. 207-8.

2. Upton Sinclair, *The Goose Step* (Pasadena, California: published by the author, 1923), p. 18.

3. M. A. Brannon, "The Montana System of Administering Higher Education," *School and Society,* XXXV (February 27, 1932), 270.

CHAPTER 4

Purdue University

"Purdue has honored me," Elliott told the Purdue University Board of Trustees on Tuesday, May 16, 1922, "I will endeavor to honor Purdue University," With these measured words, he concluded his formal response to the board's unanimous vote and thereby became the sixth president of the University.

Although Elliott was not to assume the office until September 1, 1922, the faculty was assembled in Fowler Hall by 4:00 p.m. that same day to meet the new president on his first visit to the Lafayette community. Professor Stanley Coulter, dean of the School of Science, presided at the gathering and introduced Elliott to the group. Most of the board members were present as was Governor Warren T. McCray, but none of the officials made a speech and the meeting was adjourned almost immediately in order that Elliott could be personally greeted by the various deans, heads of departments, and other members of the faculty.

Elliott remained in Lafayette for only a few days and spent most of his time talking with Dean Coulter, board members Henry W. Marshall and David E. Ross, and others about university affairs as well as about various personal matters related to his moving to the community.

On Friday the student newspaper, *The Purdue Exponent,* carried his greeting to Purdue students. "The generous welcome of the University," he declared, "has convinced me that I am to be most happy in my new responsibility. Every moment on the campus brings new and inspiring evidences of the distinction of the students of Purdue—their traditions, their loyalty, and their ideals."

That same afternoon Elliott accompanied Marshall to the Purdue-Notre Dame baseball game where Elliott shook hands and talked with several students, pitched the first ball, and stayed for the entire game. He was relaxed, enjoying himself immensely, and the students were delighted to know that the new president was a baseball fan.

THE SITUATION AT PURDUE

Purdue University in 1922 was widely recognized for its outstanding schools of engineering and agriculture. Nearing its fiftieth year of operation, the university had established itself as a vigorous and growing institution. The enrollment had been steadily increasing since 1900, and the total student population was slightly more than 3,000. Local Purdue historians, Professors William M. Hepburn and Louis M. Sears, writing at that time, noted that the institution was "an educational organism of extraordinary vigor for which the future held abundant promise."[1] It was Indiana's land-grant college, established and located apart from Indiana University at Bloomington.

Unlike the situation in Montana, where the state higher educational institutions had been competitors in every sense, there apparently existed in Indiana at that time a mutual feeling of respect between Indiana University and Purdue. Hepburn and Sears reported that there was a recognition of the essential unity of educational endeavor and there was a determination on the part of each instituion to waste no time or strength in opposition to the other's program.

In other respects the new situation was also unlike the one that had existed in Montana six years earlier. The tensions that had been evident among those who were responsible for the control and direction of the University of Montana were apparently not present at Purdue University; nor was the university under any particular pressure from the legislature to reduce spending.

As one member of the Purdue Board of Trustees wrote to Elliott, "in most cases, when a new president comes on a campus to begin his service, he does so handicapped in many ways. Often times it is because his predecessor has been discharged, because of differences in the faculty, or matters of policy in the Board of Trustees. Nothing of the kind exists here. The conditions are as nearly ideal, for the beginning of your work, as can be found any place."

Elliott's predecessor at Purdue, Winthrop E. Stone, had fallen to his death while climbing Mount Eon in the Canadian Rockies on July 17, 1921. Upon learning of Stone's untimely death, Joseph D. Oliver of South Bend, president of Purdue's Board of Trustees, immediately called Henry W. Marshall of Lafayette, chairman of the executive committee of the board, to look after matters on the campus until action could be taken to handle the day-to-day operation of the university. At a special meeting called for August 4, 1921, the board voted to suspend the rules in order that an office of "Vice President of the University" could be established. Following this action Marshall was named vice president to serve as acting president while the board searched for the new president.

Oliver appointed a committee at that meeting to assemble facts regarding every possible candidate for the presidency. Serving on the committee were, in addition to Oliver, the two other members of the executive committee, Marshall and James W. Noel of Indianapolis, and two alumni members of the board, David E. Ross of Lafayette and Perry H. Crane of Lebanon.

Oliver was the most active of the search committee members, although Marshall and Noel were of considerable assistance. They visited with university presidents in neighboring states and, accompanied by Ross and John A. Hillenbrand, travelled to New York and Washington to discuss possible candidates. The search was finally narrowed to four individuals whose names had been submitted by the General Education Board. After eight months of work, at a regular meeting of the board on April 21, 1922, Marshall moved that Oliver be authorized to invite one of those four, Edward Charles Elliott, to become president of Purdue; he was the only candidate ever presented for a vote and the motion received unanimous approval.

Elliott, of course, had written to a number of his friends in the profession as soon as he had been approached by the Purdue officials. President Nicholas Murray Butler of Columbia University and President Henry S. Pritchett of the Carnegie Foundation for the Advancement of Teaching had both written encouraging letters, but even more favorable was the report from Samuel Capen of the American Council on Education. Capen had been suggested for the position at Purdue but had declined to be considered for personal reasons which he explained to Elliott. Nevertheless he wrote that Purdue was a wonderful institution in spirit, solidity, reputation, and support. It was ready to go at full speed under the direction of a leader who knew where and how to steer it. Capen concluded that an educational renaissance was due in the state of Indiana. "Except for the limitations on the scope of the institution there is nothing better in the United States—at least nothing better has come under my eye," wrote Capen.

The most direct answer to Elliott's questions, though, came from his old friend Henry Suzzalo of the University of Washington, who wrote, "I think that you ought to accept . . . and I so advise you with all my heart." In a later letter he argued that the Purdue appointment promised to be a better situation for Elliott both personally and professionally, and most of all for the Elliott family.

Suzzalo also suggested that Elliott should have in mind a number of terms which could be agreed upon before he would want to accept the new position. Elliott, of course, had prepared such a list of ten conditions in 1915 at the time he was being considered for the chancellorship in Montana. Since these had been accepted and had proved to be of such value to the chancellor, he was easily disposed to prepare a second list for consideration by the Purdue Board of Trustees in 1922.

His new list, changed and enlarged somewhat, included the following understandings: that his appointment was to be for an indefinite term, unanimously approved by the board and by the principal officers and the members of the staff; moving expenses from Helena to Lafayette (estimated at $1,800) were guaranteed and the salary was to be set at "not less than $12,000" with one month annual vacation; the university was to provide a residence suitable as a home and for meeting the official social requirements of the presidency together with an expense account to cover the cost of such "official entertaining"; all traveling expenses incurred in connection with his duties were to be borne by the university.

Two other items were of particular interest. It was agreed that "the initiative for all nominations for the appointments, and all recommendations for the compensation, promotion, transfer, or dismissal of members of the instructional and scientific staff of the university, and all other employees of the institution, shall rest with the president acting with the advice of the administrative officers immediately concerned." And, second, "the board . . . (has) . . . primary responsibility for the financial and public policies of the university, but the president, with the aid of the faculty, has the responsibility for distinctly educational policies."

Thus, with his friends' recommendations in mind, and his list of fourteen conditions in hand, Elliott met with the board for the first time at the May meeting referred to earlier. At the afternoon session he presented his memorandum outlining the stipulations. Following the discussion, the board accepted all his terms except that the salary was to be $10,000, the same as he was receiving in Montana. The dollar item was no deterrent, particularly since he was to be provided with a house, and he eagerly began that work which was to continue for nearly a quarter of a century.

In Elliott's view, the board's willingness to review carefully these considerations, coupled with the fact that the physical demands on the president were not so strenuous, promised him an opportunity for a useful career. In a quiet, purposeful manner, he set out to direct the future growth of Indiana's land-grant institution. He requested that no inaugural ceremony be held, and was quoted as saying that he wanted to avoid the expenditures necessary for such exercises; he preferred to be inaugurated by work rather than display, he said.

The Elliott family moved to Lafayette under somewhat trying circumstances because the university had no "official residence" for its presidents. Mrs. Elliott was concerned about the size of whatever house was selected because of their four children, John (14), Susanne (11), Marion (9), and Ed (7); and because her mother, Mrs. Nowland, was now living with the family.

Mrs. Elliott had been devoted to her parents and had taken the children to the Nowland farm near Spokane almost every summer since her marriage. When her father died in April 1919, her mother, known to the family as "Granny," moved in with the Elliotts (where she made her home until she died in March 1947, on the eve of her 95th birthday).

Nothing could be done to avoid the necessity of a second move at some later date, however, and temporary arrangements were made during the summer for the forty-seven-year-old president and his family to move into a grey stucco house at 500 University Street. Located just north of the Armory, it served as the Elliott home until August 1, 1923.

The board had discussed the matter of building a new home for the president of the university and preliminary plans were made for an official residence to be constructed which would have faced Grant Street, located between the Civil Engineering building and the Purdue Memorial Union. Elliott and Mrs. Elliott, however, were not particularly pleased with the thought of having their residence on campus. Then when the preliminary cost estimates were presented to the board, there was general agreement that the price was too high and that locating the president's house on the campus might interfere with an orderly campus development of classroom buildings. The situation was relieved in April 1923, when the board decided to purchase and refurbish Dr. Guy Levering's residence at 515 South Seventh Street in Lafayette.

More than two miles from the campus and Elliott's office in Fowler Hall, the location presented Elliott with an opportunity to indulge himself daily in his favorite exercise, walking. In Montana he and son John had frequently gone on weekend hikes, sometimes for 10 to 15 miles in rugged mountain country; occasionally the whole family went for much shorter jaunts. In Lafayette he immediately began the practice of walking briskly to and from the campus, spurning the frequent offers of a ride. Not only did he enjoy it, but it was in keeping with his Montana physician's suggestion that he would have less "stomach trouble" if he could schedule a daily walk in the open. The daily ritual soon became a local legend and there probably always will be frequent references to Elliott's erect stride when his personal traits are discussed by those who knew him at Purdue.

THE INAUGURAL YEAR IN INDIANA

During his inaugural year, Elliott carefully limited the number of speaking engagements and spent most of his time learning more about the institution. Just six days after he officially took office, however, Elliott spoke in Indianapolis before a Purdue Alumni Association meeting, outlining some of his ideas concerning the presidency. After pledging himself to serve the people of Indiana, he briefly discussed student life, the physical welfare of students, and the athletic program, then carefully expressed a belief which he had originally phrased for his inaugural address at Montana. He came to use this theme over and over when he addressed various groups in order to provide his listeners with a statement of his acknowledged responsibilities as president of Purdue. He called this paragraph his "Personal Charter," or later, the "Purdue Philosophy" and it appeared in print with slight changes more than a dozen times:

> As President of Purdue I will not consider that I have met my responsibilities until the leadership and the citizenship of the state of Indiana, of whatever class or occupation, continue to recognize that this university is their university; that Purdue University is an integral part of the public school system of the State ever working in its own distinctive and assigned fields; that Purdue is a worthy

agency, ever at their disposal for aiding them to meet the needs that determine the happiness, the satisfaction and the ideals of their lives; until there is firmly established among students and teachers and alumni the enduring principle that the daily work of men makes education possible, and that education in turn must make the daily work of men possible and pleasurable.

At that same Indianapolis alumni dinner in the Hotel Lincoln, board member Henry Marshall announced that George Ade, '87, and David Ross, '93, had given 65 acres of land lying northwest of the campus to the university to be used as an athletic field and playground for the students of Purdue. Marshall noted that "the topography of the land is ideal for a beautiful stadium as well as football and baseball fields, tennis courts, and a golf links." The purchase price was forty thousand dollars, and Purdue's Ross-Ade Stadium was soon under construction. Today that valuable property is being used almost exactly as the donors envisioned, as an intercollegiate sports center for the Purdue teams that developed and gained national prominence during the late twenties and the thirties, the so-called "golden age of sports."

The first football game of the 1922 season was with Millikin College, Saturday, October 7. On the preceding night Elliott attended and addressed the pep session. After the band had played, he spoke of the future of Purdue athletics and, with his sleeves rolled, Elliott urged the students to get behind their team and give it "the push that will send it on to victory. In a sense our future in athletics is tied up in tomorrow's game," he said, "and we will not be disappointed."

Elliott's rolled shirt sleeves made a hit with the student body and on the Saturday morning of the game, the *Exponent* printed an editorial headed "Things That The Pep Session Revealed:"

> . . . we have in President Elliott a colleague, a co-worker, and a fellow booster of Purdue. One who is not afraid to strip off his coat and take the stage in his shirt sleeves, and yell and cheer as much as anyone. He even turned poet for the occasion. President Elliott has done everything in his power to boost athletics and he would even venture to lead a cheer or play end on the team if the occasion demanded it.

At an October 1922 board meeting, Elliott asked for and received permission to engage consultants to develop a campus plan which would provide for the orderly development of the campus, giving special attention to the placement of streets, walkways, buildings, and landscaping. Subsequently, the Lafayette firm of Nicol, Scholer, and Hoffman was engaged and prepared a campus plan which was approved by the board in April 1924.

In November 1922, it was announced that the university had employed its first comptroller and business manager, W. T. Middlebrook of Griffenhager and Associates, Ltd. With the appointment of Middlebrook, the university began to develop a new accounting system and to operate on a strict budget basis. This led ultimately to the development of a central purchasing office, a continuing inventory of university property, and a host of fiscal controls which put the university on a firm, business-like basis which was to be of immeasurable assistance to the university as it dealt with legislators and legislative committees of the future.

Elliott's first year was an unbelievably busy one. On November 25, 1922, he laid the cornerstone of the Purdue Memorial Union building during Homecoming exercises. In January 1923, he proposed to the board that each staff member be required annually to prepare a "service report form" which would give the administration an opportunity to review the performance of each individual staff member. The board approved without dissent.

He visited alumni groups in Chicago, Detroit, Washington, D.C., Buffalo, Niagara Falls, New York City, Cincinnati, Indianapolis, and other lesser cities. At an alumni meeting in Cleveland, two Purdue boosters who met Elliott's train were dismayed at his appearance. He was wearing high-button shoes and a rough textured suit which, although it may have been in style in Helena, had the appearance in Cleveland of being several years old. The two hosts were more than a little disturbed by what they saw. Following the dinner meeting, however, Elliott's stirring speech convinced the group that the new president was a great one. The two alums who had been reluctant to introduce Elliott to their friends, were, by the time the evening was over, eager to be associated with Elliott as members of the host committee.

Elliott worked diligently to get acquainted with the alumni and to learn what they had to say about Purdue. He attended faculty meetings, board meetings, and many of the student gatherings as well as athletic events in order to learn more about the university. His future at Purdue was an exciting challenge, and he was concerned with all aspects of university life. He set out to become closely identified with students, parents and alumni, professors and administrators, public officials, and the citizenry of the state.

THE SEMI-CENTENNIAL YEAR—1924

Even before Elliott had been elected to the presidency, Purdue officials had started planning for a series of events to mark the fiftieth year of university operation, and the new president (who was also to reach his fiftieth year in 1924) was soon actively engaged in helping to organize and arrange appropriate ceremonies.

Those most involved in the planning, of course, were the four deans, distinguished individuals who were acknowledged leaders in the university: Stanley Coulter, dean of the School of Science and dean of men; Carolyn E. Shoemaker, dean of women; J. H. Skinner, dean of the School of Agriculture; and A. A. Potter, dean of the Schools of Engineering. But the general format and the speakers who were selected indicated that Elliott had directly influenced the arrangements.

The celebration extended over a three day period, May 1-3, 1924, and included addresses by Elliott's long time friends, President E. A. Birge of the University of Wisconsin, President William Oxley Thompson of Ohio State University, and President Henry Suzzalo of the University of Washington. A complete account of the semi-centennial, which was later published,[2] included reprints of the major addresses; the event was to Elliott the outstanding happening of the year.

Elliott presided at various exercises but his major address, "The Pursuit of Power," was delivered before the assemblage on May 3, 1924. It was his most important address of the year and was probably designed to a certain extent to take the place of an inaugural address. In the opening paragraph he noted that in his view, Purdue University owed its life

> to the belief that labor and learning, intelligence and industry are inseparable in any form of society where men count themselves free. With the founding of that group of American institutions, of which Purdue University is but a single representative, the potential of all education was immeasurably increased for free men and their descendants whose destiny is work.

The problems of Purdue, he said, were primarily problems of the campus, although as an integral part of the public school system of the state, Purdue had an inescapable responsibility to the public elementary and secondary schools of the state.

He declared that more adequate living accommodations should be provided for the student body and hoped that the university would be able to provide housing facilities under its own control. He indicated that there were social and educational problems which were centered in the college fraternity houses, although several years later wrote that "the fraternities as a whole are genuine educational assets." (But in 1940 after several university-operated residence halls for both men and women had been erected at Purdue, he wrote, "I crave the day when similar physical facilities and educational advantages may be offered to all Purdue students.")

During this talk, he made brief reference to a plan for reorganizing the curricula so that students of ability and persistence could complete work for the degree in three years instead of four; or that students who were obliged to be self-supporting could have the opportunity of completing their work with dignity and success through a period of more than four years. Although Elliott did not make reference to this suggestion again before any large group, he frequently talked and wrote about the importance of providing for individual differences during the months that followed the semi-centennial celebration. He included this item, for example, in his review of the year 1923-1924, his second year as president of Purdue.

During his first two years in office his critical examination of the internal affairs of the university revealed ten problems. Among those problems were the matter of housing of students, student social life, a better and more comprehensive plan of physical education, and the development of ways to provide for individual student differences. For the faculty he hoped for better coordination of instruction, research, and extension, as well as the reorganization of the faculty so as to minimize the demands for administrative service from persons on the teaching and research staff. From the administration he hoped for better scheduling of classes so as to secure more economic utilization of buildings and facilities and he wanted more systematic and better supervision of instruction. Finally, he hoped for a further consolidation of alumni interests with the essential interests of the university.

The largest single problem was that of obtaining financial support commensurate with the enlarging needs of the university, he said.

The University did not create these needs. They have been developed with our evolving civilization. Our people, our agriculture, our industries, our culture, expects more and more from the institution and its workers. The State must do more for the University. The University will always do more for the State.

After two years on the campus, Elliott was setting the pattern of work for his administration. He had outlined some of the immediate goals and was working to set up an administrative organization to handle the problems. By this time, Hepburn and Sears had analyzed the personality of Elliott as

. . . one of restless energy and force, dynamic in a word, and one that gives assurance of large vision and a will to overcome all obstacles. It is becoming evident to faculty and students, too, that the underlying philosophy of the new executive is individualistic. Personalities and problems are viewed in their peculiar setting. Humanity is set above administrative regulation. The temptation to classify all cases in terms of ancient ordinances is vigorously resisted.

The students awarded the 1924 "Leather Medal" to Elliott. Then as now, it was presented (annually) to the person who had done the most for the university during the past year. The problems of the campus, though, were no more important than were the problems of the state, and Elliott was soon engaged in an active study of financial affairs.

EARLY FINANCIAL PROBLEMS

The year before Elliott was elected to the presidency of Purdue University, the state legislature had made provisions for a 5 mill state tax to support higher education in Indiana; Purdue's share was 2 mills per $100 of taxable property. When Elliott reviewed the work of the legislature of 1923, he acknowledged that the university had been treated as well as could be reasonably expected and was apparently pleased to announced that there was no disposition on the part of the legislature to assume any critical or super-economical attitude.

The tax provided by the legislature of 1921 was continued through 1924, although the annual income of the University was reduced in 1923-1924 because of the reduction of the property valuation of the state. In 1923, however, the legislature did pass a special appropriation for a new heating and power plant which was needed before any plans could be made for an enlarged physical plant.

As blue prints were being drawn in 1924 for the further expension of the university, Purdue University and Indiana University, by mutually agreed action, presented budgets to the 1925 legislature based upon the doubling of the 5 mill state tax provided for in 1921; although with the further reduction of the assessed valuation of property in the state, even the proposed 10 mill state tax in 1925 probably would not have resulted in any excessive increase in university income. Elliott and Purdue were hoping for approximately $2,000,000 annually from this source.

But as Elliott later wrote, it was plainly evident, even before the opening of the legislature, that the university ". . . would be tried by the well-known political ordeal known as 'economy,'" and as a result of the economy drive, *all* state tax levies for specific purposes were abolished. In the future all state funds for the university were to be obtained through general appropriation bills, and under this plan the university was to present its case before the legislature every two years. The guarantees of the tax levy had been removed.

Writing in the March 1925, issue of the *Purdue Alumnus,* Elliott noted that a session of the legislature is always a "discouraging experience." He had campaigned vigorously in Montana for the stability of income afforded by the mill tax and had found that guarantee of funds at Purdue, only to have it abolished by the 1925 legislature.

Appropriations for the biennium were substantially the same as would have been received under the old special levy law, however, and other special appropriations were made for the construction of additional buildings; so Elliott concluded that ". . . the friends and supporters of the University are entitled to be optimistic for the future. It is perhaps better that the people of the state feel that the University is receiving too little rather than too much." Elliott announced that he would proceed to inform the people of the state concerning the needs of the university, for he felt that the case for higher education was stronger than it had ever been. "Legislators may come and go," he wrote, "but Purdue is immortal."

Although not related to the actions of the legislature regarding Purdue's financial problem, Elliott announced in July 1925, that Middlebrook had resigned as comptroller to go the University of Minnesota. He was very shortly replaced by R. B. Stewart who came to Purdue from Albion College where he had worked in a similar position. Stewart was to remain with the university as its chief financial officer throughout Elliott's tenure and beyond until his retirement in 1961.

OTHER PROBLEMS AT PURDUE

In addition to reviewing the financial problems of the university in his 1924-25 annual report, Elliott also repeated his list of ten "problems of consequence" referred to earlier and added five more. The additions included his request for the establishment of an office within the university for the "continuous, critical study of the internal mechanisms and efficiencies of the institution." Thus, the Division of Educational Reference was established at the beginning of the 1925-26 academic year largely at Elliott's insistence. He frequently referred to the agency in later years and obviously favored the kind of "impersonal, cold-blooded, constructive analysis" that he felt the division provided for the university.

Elliott also called for a reconstitution of the graduate work at the university. Although the graduate school was not established until several years later, Elliott was making the first request for the establishment of such a school.

Another problem to which he specifically called attention was the need for some type of retirement plan for all the permanent staff members. At that time, he indicated, only about 20 percent of the staff were eligible to receive the benefits of the Carnegie Retiring Allowance and he felt the development of a more inclusive retirement plan was imperative.

He also pointed to the need for a university editor to supervise the preparation and distribution of the various university publications.

The final problem to which he called particular attention had to do with the handling of large freshmen classes. "Something radically remedial will probably need to be devised before the University will be able to promote the best interests of the individual student and at the same time protect its own standards," he noted.

Despite these internal problems, however, the financial problem resulting from the legislature's action in 1925 was still one of the larger problems facing his administration. During the months that followed the legislative session there was much concern among various groups who apparently were pressing for a solution to the problems of finance.

THE STATE SURVEY

As a result of these pressures, in May 1926, Governor Ed Jackson, who had taken office in 1925, announced that a state survey would be made to examine the work and needs of Purdue University, Indiana University, and the two state normal schools. The original memorandum announced that it seemed imperative that all the determining facts relative to the financial needs of the state's universities and normal schools be brought to the surface. A list of nine questions was included in the memorandum for the survey commission to attempt to answer.

A survey staff was appointed which included Elliott's long-time friend, Charles Judd of the University of Chicago, as director; Floyd W. Reeves, professor of education at the University of Kentucky; and others.

When the survey report was completed in December 1926,[3] the nine questions along with three others added by the commission, were answered in such a way as to indicate that the legislature had *not* provided adequate financial support, and further indicated that more money needed to be made available to the higher schools.

Thus, while the amount of appropriations made by the 1927 legislature was still below the request presented and urged in the university budget; there were certain added financial resources made available to Purdue which were encouraging to Elliott. His review of the 1926-28 biennium contained a reprint of portions of the survey report and concluded that the survey "contributed appreciably to the favorable and constructive attitude which prevailed during the 1927 legislative session."

The 1927 legislature passed an act levying a special 2 mill tax for a building fund which came to be known as the "educational improvement fund" and promised to bring $350,000 annually to Purdue. In addition, the legislature authorized the board of trustees to issue bonds for the purpose of erecting and furnishing student dormitories, an act which Elliott hailed as enabling the university " . . . to begin the realization of the long discussed plan of providing essential living facilities for students." The authorization was a signal achievement which opened the way for future growth by providing a new kind of financing.

Two years before, at the close of the 1925-26 academic year, Elliott had selected the state survey as one of four items for special mention in his annual report; the actions of the 1927 legislature indicated that he had picked a significant activity.

At the same time (1926), he had written of another event which he thought might " . . . prove to be the most important event of the University year." The event was the Conference of Industrial Leaders of the state, held at the university on June 1, 1926, under the direction of David E. Ross, then vice president of the board of trustees. The aim of the conference was to center attention upon a program of research for the further development of the industries and of the natural resources of the state. It proved to be the conference that led to the development of an allied corporation which has contributed immeasurably to the growth and development of Purdue University—the Purdue Research Foundation.

THE ALLIED CORPORATIONS

Before an attempt is made to write of the Purdue Research Foundation, however, it may be well to review the origin of the first allied corporation established at Purdue in 1923, the RossAde Foundation. In later years, the Purdue Research Foundation (1930), Better Homes in America (1935), the Purdue Aeronautics Corporation (1942), and others were also incorporated to serve as agencies to stimulate and support certain special activities.

The Ross-Ade Foundation, the first to be established, traced its history back to 1922 when David E. Ross and George Ade, both prominent alumni of Purdue, the former a member of the board of trustees, acquired the tract of land referred to earlier which they proposed to give to the university for a recreational field and a site for an athletic stadium.

Under the existing laws, however, the university could not assume bond issues to develop the tract of land; it would have had to rely on state appropriations or gifts to provide suitable buildings and other facilities for the area. Thus the proposed gift raised a number of problems when consideration was given to the further development of the acreage.

According to several sources, Elliott suggested to the donors that a separate corporation could be established, controlled by the university, which would prevent putting financial obligation on the University itself. The plan met with the approval of the donors and the trustees, and the Ross-Ade Foundation was incorporated on November 26, 1923, under the laws of Indiana with Elliott as president.

By the articles of incorporation the foundation was to promote educational purposes in connection with Purdue University by providing money for the needs of the university with particular reference to buildings, grounds, or other suitable facilities or equipment for the physical, recreational, or athletic needs of Purdue's students or to provide educational facilities for the military training of those students.

The foundation has since proved its usefulness many times over. In addition to the Ross-Ade Stadium it has held title to land for an engineering camp, a 4-H center, various farm tracts, land for a group of residence halls, and other properties. But perhaps the Ross-Ade Foundation is most valuable because it was the first of four agencies which were legal devices for accomplishing that which probably could not otherwise have been accomplished.

The second agency to be established, the Purdue Research Foundation, was the one destined to lead the others in practically every respect, and its development is closely related to the organization of the Department of Research Relations with Industry. Elliott was aware that the rapid growth of the university's engineering schools had brought prominent men in industry to the campus in increasing numbers. As a consequence, industry had become more aware of the potential worth of the university and was asking for university help toward the solution of some of industry's most troublesome problems. Upon considering these demands for fundamental education and research, the trustees were investigating the possibility of establishing an all-university department which could devote all its time and energies to the development of a better relationship between industry and the university.

David Ross, who had been elected president of the board of trustees in the summer of 1927 to succeed Marshall, (J. D. Oliver had resigned in 1924), was particularly eager to develop a plan for industrial research at Purdue. In April 1926, while he was vice president of the board, he had recommended that a committee be appointed to study the problem, and set out to organize a conference of industrial leaders to be held at Purdue.

The conference on June 1, 1926, was attended by industrial leaders of many states, all guests of David Ross. Elliott's address before the group of industrialists centered on a proposal to provide an advisory committee which would establish a connecting link between the research laboratories of the university and the problems of Indiana industries. It seemed to Elliott that the industries of the state might well develop a plan for scientific cooperation with the university similar to that developed by the agricultural interests in 1909 when an advisory committee was established for the Purdue Agricultural Experiment Station.

Though no special action was taken either by the board or by the conference group, Elliott and Ross had made it clear that the university was interested in the problems of industry.

During the months both before and after the event, Ross, frequently accompanied by Dean Potter, spent much of his time visiting the principal research laboratories of the country, several universities, and a number of large industrial organizations to try to find out how Purdue could better serve the industries of the state. Almost a year later Ross made an elaborate report to the trustees urging greater attention to the problem. Ross who had retired as vice president and general manager of Ross Gear and Tool Company was eager to devote virtually all of his energies and money to Purdue. According to his biographer, Fred Kelly, "to improve Purdue was more than a chief interest to Dave. It became a consuming passion."[4]

Later in 1927, Elliott placed before the trustees a plan for the creation of a Department of Research Relations with Industry to become effective May 1, 1928. The board approved Elliott's recommendation on October 12, 1927. The first director of research relations with industry employed by Elliott, G. Stanley Meikle, made an extensive survey of Indiana industrialists in 1928 to determine what procedures should be followed. Industries' doors had been opened for him by the previous visits of Dave Ross and Potter. Elliott, Ross and Meikle concluded that the progressive industrialist was far more interested in having the university intensively develop creative thinkers capable of solving problems than he was in having the university solve the problems.[5]

When it became apparent that industry would provide financial support for a cooperative effort to find and train individuals with creative ability, the department was able to set its course. The major objectives, as outlined by Elliott, were: (1) the discovery and intensive training of creative thinkers; (2) the use of fundamental research as a joint enterprise in education; (3) the development of more adequate research facilities and of well-trained personnel; (4) the development of a policy which would lead to cordial and sympathetic relationships between industry and the university; and (5) the accumulation of funds necessary to carry on research as an educational function.

Within a very short time after the department was established, however, it became evident that there were many problems associated with the development of fundamental research that could not easily be handled by the university. Such problems included the assignment, protection, and defense of patentable discoveries; the protection of student and staff members against exploitation; and the safeguarding of venture capital provided by grants, trusts, or outright gifts. Once again the answer seemed to depend upon a separate corporation, controlled by the university, which would prevent putting financial obligation on the university itself. As a result, the Purdue Research Foundation was incorporated on December 30, 1930, by all of the members of the board of trustees and the president of the university. David Ross and board member J. K. Lilly of Indianapolis were the first contributors.

More than a decade later Elliott wrote that the foundation had more than proved the usefulness and the soundness of its basic ideas. In addition to its initial purposes, the agency, according to Elliott, came to serve " . . . as an instrument for effective two-way communication from the University to the outside world, and from this world to the University. Each gain from this exchange of power."

Two years after the establishment of the Purdue Research Foundation, at the Third Industrial Research Conference, Elliott took the opportunity to develop and elaborate on an idea which he had first expressed seven years earlier in an address before the National Education Association in 1925. His comments, reported below, are typically Elliott in tone and may well have been one of his most significant statements regarding higher education in America.

Political enemies may attempt to undermine, critics may cavil, bigots may bluster, but the cold, indisputable fact remains that higher education, during the quarter of century just passing, has furnished more than ever before the germinal nuclei for the permanency and the potency of the doctrine of human opportunity; and has become a great driving force for the advance of both material and spiritual things.

Our existing organization for higher education represents a process of continual flowering of human destiny through, by, and for opportunity. Whether we pursue the route of sentimental aspiration, or that of stern statistics, we inevitably reach the conclusion that what we, as a people . . . , and what we are accomplishing for the cause of civilization, are more directly the products of the services and the skills of our colleges, our universities, and our professional schools, than of any other existing agency or group of

existing agencies. These institutions distinctly . . . embody the
best of our American idealism, the firmest of our confidence in the
present, and the most stable of our faith in the future. They,
above all, have been the means for giving a human reality to
ideals.

His talk was entitled "Dollars for Ideals; Ideals for Dividends"
and it was Elliott's judgment, unquestionably, that the Purdue
Research Foundation was one of the most important agencies that
permitted the university to transmit dollars to ideals and ideals
to dividends.

In December 1923, Better Homes in America was incorporated
in Delaware with Herbert Hoover, then Secretary of Commerce,
as its first president. Mrs. William Brown Meloney of New York
was generally credited with initiating and promoting the organization whose activities were designed to promote and encourage
the building and maintenance of better homes throughout America by conducting educational campaigns, research, and programs
of every kind to improve the design and construction of homes,
their surroundings, decoration, and furnishings and equipment.
The influence of Better Homes in America spread throughout the
country during the dozen years following 1923. Nearly 5,000 local
committees were organized to work in communities with reference to the various aspects of home improvement. Supporting
funds were largely obtained from civic-minded benefactors.

In 1932 the national office was moved from Washington, D.C.,
to New York City, but three years later (1935) Elliott was asked if
the organization could be placed under the sponsorship of Purdue University. Elliott believed that Purdue, as a land-grant college, had been established by men who saw in modern science a
"limitless power for the promotion of human welfare." Therefore,
anything that the university could do to raise the standard of
living of the common people of the nation was well within the
responsibility of the university. The concept was approved by the
trustees, and in 1935, Better Homes in America was reincorporated
under the laws of Indiana, and all the records, books, data, publications, and files were transferred to the new corporation.

The nation was in the throes of the great depression and Elliott, noting that housing was one of the most depressed of all
of the industries, reasoned that housing construction offered the
most immediate as well as the most long-lasting opportunity for
the "re-energizing of the durable goods industries." At a Homes
Conference held at Purdue, Elliott reported that there were ". . .

two million families with annual incomes of $2,500, a large proportion of whom would be prospective purchasers of homes if a well-built 5-room house, complete with adequate land, improvements, and accessories could be acquired for $5,000 or less."

The Purdue Research Foundation served as the agency under which the Purdue Housing Research Program was established, and a number of experimental houses were constructed adjacent to the campus. Within a year these three bedroom homes had been planned and constructed with the cooperation of industry at a unit cost of $5,000 and yet a "decent minimum of quality" had been maintained. David Ross, through the Purdue Research Foundation, had provided some of the funds for this initial venture into the field of housing but additional funds were not readily available. Elliott found it difficult to accept the fact that it was virtually impossible to secure funds for research in this home building activity. "The automobile industry, the electrical industry, even the food industry," he said, "spend many times that amount annually for the improvement of their product. But because the housing business is apparently everybody's business and likewise nobody's responsibility, we continue the processes and practices of the horse and buggy age."

During the next few years it became increasingly apparent that adequate funds would probably not be provided to carry out the rather elaborate plans for housing research. Finally, at a meeting of the board of directors on August 5, 1943, it was voted to suspend the operation of the corporation for the duration of the war. The project was never reactivated.

The Purdue Aeronautics Corporation, another allied corporation, was established in 1942 to further the development of aeronautical engineering and to provide for the more effective utilization of the Purdue University Airport. The airport, owned by the Purdue Research Foundation, had begun its operation in 1930 when Ross purchased more than 100 acres of land and turned it over to the foundation as an airport facility. On the day that government officials visited the site, November 1, 1930, a landing ring and a wind sock were installed and with this act the Purdue University Airport was established. Not until four years later was ground broken for the first hangar.

Elliott had a continuing interest in the airport and in promoting the aeronautics program at Purdue which was evident in a variety of ways. His most publicized act, of course, was that of naming Amelia Earhart to a newly-created position as consultant in careers for women in 1935.

Shortly after the Purdue Aeronautics Corporation was established, Elliott testified before a senate subcommittee that he thought land-grant colleges could perform the same services to aviation that had been rendered to agriculture indicating that perhaps aviation, in the years to come, was going to be just as important to the nation as agriculture had been in the last two generations. The Purdue Aeronautics Corporation, without question, has had a major role in the development of airport facilities and equipment.

Elliott's interest in these allied corporations extended over the entire term of his presidency; but the pattern for these "legal agencies" was established during his first ten years in office.

THE DECADE—1922-1932

As Elliott neared the end of his first decade at Purdue, he continued to travel over the country visiting alumni groups, encouraging their continued support. Although he had visited virtually every major city in the East and in the Midwest, it was not until 1928 that he made his first extended trip to the Western states.

At about the time he announced his plans to make the trip, several members of the board agreed among themselves that Elliott had more than proved his worth to the university. So at an April board meeting, while Elliott was out of the room, board president Dave Ross led a discussion relative to Elliott's six-year tenure with Purdue, pointing out that three years earlier, in April 1925, they had increased his salary to $12,000. When the president was called back to the meeting, Ross told him that the board had contributed $500 in order that Elliott's portrait could be painted, then said, "It gives me great pleasure to tell you also that by unanimous vote the board has raised your salary to $15,000 effective at the beginning of the next fiscal year."

Although Elliott's exact words were not recorded, the secretary of the board noted in the minutes that "Elliott expressed his deep appreciation for the board's generous recognition of his services, which he could not accept, as he did not think the financial condition of the University justified such an increase at this time."

So Elliott declined the salary increase although he did reluctantly consent to having his portrait painted. (One year later, however, in April 1929, the board voted unanimously to set Elliott's salary at $15,000 effective April 1, 1929. This time the item was not a matter for discussion with the president; it was presented to him as an accomplished fact.)

Then on May 22, 1928, Elliott left Lafayette to spend 24 days "lining up" Purdue alumni groups along the West Coast. In 24 days Elliott attended 24 banquets, most of them given by Purdue alumni clubs. Alumni were visited in Chicago, Omaha, Los Angeles, San Francisco, Portland, Seattle, Spokane, Minneapolis, Milwaukee, and elsewhere. For the first time since he had left Helena in 1922, the former chancellor of the University of Montana visited his old headquarters. Taking note of this trip, George Ade, a distinguished Purdue alumnus who was serving as guest editor for *The Purdue Alumnus,* reported that "Purdue has never had a more cheerful emissary or one who sets out on a pilgrimage with a more definite purpose."

His visitations apparently were most successful, for in September 1928, Lawrence Downs, president of the Illinois Central Railroad and a Purdue graduate, said at the first student convocation of the year that Elliott was "the greatest man the country has produced for such a position. I hope that Dr. Elliott will stay here the rest of his life and that no other school will be able to gobble him up."

In order to keep in close contact with the alumni, Elliott began writing a one-page feature article for each issue of *The Purdue Alumnus* in October 1929. He called it "The President's Page", and continued it for the next five years, finally dropping it as a regular feature in June 1934. During all his years in the presidency, however, he penned at least one message annually to the alumni.

How did they respond? In May 1929, during Gala Week, the alumni presented him with a new Packard sedan to replace the first car he ever owned, a rather delapidated 1919 Hudson Super Six touring car. He proudly drove the Packard until May 1, 1937, at which time he was presented with a second new Packard sedan by the alumni group. His affection for this automobile was such that he kept it until several years after he had retired as president.

Also in the spring of 1929, Elliott received his third honorary degree, a Doctor of Laws, from Columbia University as a feature of Columbia's 175th anniversary of its founding (his previous honorary degrees having been awarded by DePauw University and Butler University the preceding year). Honored with him at Columbia in 1929 were three other college presidents who were good friends: Lotus D. Coffman, the University of Minnesota; Walter A. Jessup, the University of Iowa, and Livingston Farrant, Cornell University.

Having gained the rather widespread general respect and support of the alumni and the citizens of the state, Elliott was disposed to present the ever-recurring problems of financial support to the people. So in 1930, in order to get the matter before the graduates of Purdue and others, Elliott prepared an account for the *Purdue Alumnus* in which he attempted to present the heart of the financial problem. For a number of years, he wrote, the appropriations made for the support and physical growth had been far from meeting the needs of the institution. While the enrollment had increased from about 3,000 students in 1924 to more than 4,500 in 1930, the legislative appropriations had not kept pace. According to Elliott the university had "practically exhausted its reserve of supplies and equipment." He acknowledged that the existing emergency in the affairs of the state at that time dictated an attempt at economy, but the youth of Indiana should have as good an opportunity for education and advancement as that provided by any other state in the Union. Reiterating this theme, he campaigned vigorously during the months preceding the 1931 meeting of the legislature.

Harry G. Leslie, a Purdue graduate who had served as executive secretary of the Purdue Alumni Association from 1924 to 1928, had been elected governor of Indiana and had taken office in January 1929. With the governor's office and many members of the legislature solidly behind the two state universities, the 1931 legislature eventually approved the budgets as prepared by university officials, and the financial problems for the next biennium were no longer an item of great concern.

During the months that followed, Elliott turned part of his attention to a plan for reviewing the changes and progress that had taken place at Purdue during the decade 1922-1932.

September 30, 1932, was the date marking the end of Purdue's 58th year of operation, but as Elliott wrote, it represented "something more than merely the time for the official closing of another of the series of annual records. It was the decennial of my own service to the institution. This circumstance naturally resulted in a disposition to review and to evaluate the institutional changes that have taken place during recent years."

Thus in December 1931, Elliott sent a memorandum to the various administrative officers, announcing that the university planned to publish a review of the decade in the fall of 1932. Of the four deans who had been at Purdue in 1922, three were still distinguished academic leaders: Dean Shoemaker, Dean Skinner, and Dean Potter. But Dean Coulter had retired in 1926, and M. L. Fisher had replaced him as dean of men while R. B. Moore had taken over the responsibilities of dean of the School of Science. Dean Moore died, however, before the close of the decade and H. E. Enders became dean of the school in March 1932.

Among others to whom Elliott turned for facts about the preceding ten years were C. B. Jordan, appointed dean of the new School of Pharmacy in 1924; Mary L. Mathews, named dean of the new School of Home Economics in 1926; R. G. Dukes, first dean of the Graduate School, appointed in 1929; Director G. I. Christie of the Agricultural Experiment Station; Director N. A. Kellogg, Department of Athletics; and, of course, Librarian W. M. Hepburn and University Editor R. W. Babcock. Elliott indicated that the project appealed to him as an exceptional opportunity to assess the events and accomplishments of the immediate past, and perhaps could be used as a background for the planning of the next decade.

The task of digesting and editing the reports from university officials fell to Babcock; the part dealing with financial administration and physical development was assigned to R. B. Stewart, comptroller of the University. The volume, entitled *Purdue University, 1922-1932,* was published in September 1933.[6] It stands as a valuable historical account of university development during the ten-year period.

Most of the changes described as having taken place had been specifically mentioned by Elliott in his annual reviews of the year, but the following items, for example, were cited again as significant developments:

1. The discontinuance of the three-year course in pharmacy.

2. The establishment of a degree course in physical education.

3. The adoption of a faculty report on the social and moral needs of students.

4. The organization of the graduate work of the university into the Graduate School and the appointment of R. G. Dukes as dean.

5. The development of the Department of Research Relations with Industry and the establishment of the Purdue Research Foundation.

6. The adoption of a long-range campus plan and the inauguration of the physical plant extension program made possible by the "educational improvement fund" established by the 1927 legislature.

7. The reorganization of the control of the Purdue Memorial Union, thus permitting the beginning of the completion of the structure.

8. The opening of Franklin Levering Cary Hall, the new residence hall for men.

An article in the *Purdue Alumnus,* which praised Elliott highly, noted that since 1922 the university had named a comptroller and moved to a budget plan for fiscal administration; that buildings constructed since 1922 represented approximately 60 per cent of the value of all Purdue buildings; the enrollment had gone from about 3,000 students in 1921-22 to approximately 5,500 in 1931-32. The author of the article, staff member T. R. Johnston, wrote, however, that the greatest contribution of the university's dynamic president was to "the new spirit of Purdue."

Some of the faculty members who had been on the campus since 1922 might have recalled with some asperity that six months after Elliott had assumed the presidency, he had written to deans, directors, and department heads noting that in his opinion, ". . . a number of University departments are at present overstaffed; that some of the members of the instructional staff have inadequate assignments; and that the overhead costs of some departments is entirely too great." He had candidly announced that he would ". . . approve advancement of salary and rank only to those . . . for whom a demonstrated high quality of work can be exhibited."

And in 1924 he had disturbed some faculty members when he was overheard saying that ". . . everytime a student fails in his work we should examine closely to discover whether the institution was not responsible."

And again in 1926, Elliott had acted decisively when he learned that a staff member had publicly endorsed a commercial product. An advertisement for a patent medicine headed "Purdue Instructor Takes Firm Stand" had appeared in several Indiana papers. Noting that the advertisement contained a testimonial purporting to be signed by a member of the instructional staff, Elliott advised the instructor to "secure the withdrawal of the testimonial" or "relinquish his position." When he notified the board of his actions, they voted unanimously to "refuse to countenance the name of the University in connection with any commercial testimonials."

But faculty members could also recall that Elliott had recommended to the board and secured approval for regulations providing for leaves of absence (sabbatical leaves) with pay (1923), significant fee reductions for dependent children of staff members (1923), a retirement plan (1926) tied in with the Carnegie Foundation for the Advancement of Teaching which he was working to improve, and a plan for group life insurance which provided sizeable benefits (1929).

And some senior faculty members undoubtedly remembered that at a convocation held to commemorate the 125th anniversary of the birth of John Purdue on November 1, 1923, Elliott honored nine staff members who had completed thirty years service to Purdue. The following year, he brought together eighteen staff members who had served 25 years or more and cited them as members of a mythical "Purdue Twenty-Five Year Club." When Librarian Hepburn noted late in 1929 that the group had not been called together since 1924, the president and Mrs. Elliott promptly arranged a dinner at the president's home for 24 staff members who had 25 or more years of service. (But the "club" was dissolved at the Founder's Day dinner in 1933 when Elliott noted that the numbers were increasing and such a sizeable group could no longer be singled out for special recognition.)

Faculty, students, and alums were aware that an overall campus plan had been developed and that there appeared to be a guaranteed income to the building fund which would permit new construction; and it was generally known that the deans and directors had been asked to meet with the president and the board on several occasions to determine building priorities.

Anyone who was close to the university recognized that the relationships among board members and the president were excellent. Although J. D. Oliver and Henry Marshall were no longer on the board, J. W. Noel, Virginia Meredith, John A. Hillenbrand, and J. K. Lilly, along with the others, were enthusiastic and highly responsive to the leadership of board president David Ross and Elliott. Willing to work long hours, representatives of the board, starting in 1926, met with board members from the other three state institutions, for example, when budget requests were being prepared for the legislature.

Many Purdue graduates were also pleased when, at Elliott's suggestion, the faculty adopted the policy of granting honorary degrees to distinguished alumni; the first four of which were awarded on June 15, 1926, to George Ade, John T. McCutcheon, C. H. Robertson, and Chase S. Osborn. Two years later this "new spirit of Purdue" was felt in the community when the board moved to adopt the custom of holding a president's reception each fall for staff members and citizens "to promote social and educational interest in the work and life of the University."

So it seemed appropriate to Elliott and others at the close of ten years service to arrange a special ceremony to be held on May 6, 1932, to celebrate the 63rd anniversary of the founding of Purdue University; and as it turned out, this first Founder's Day Program was also a day of recognition for Elliott.

An alumni committee composed of F. F. Chandler, Burr S. Swezey, Martha Robertson, O. M. Booher, W. A. Knapp, and T. R. Johnston planned the affair. Dr. William Oxley Thompson of Ohio State University, who had been the main speaker at the semicentennial celebration at Purdue eight years previously, was selected as the speaker of the evening. Chandler was chosen toastmaster while David Ross spoke on behalf of the Board of Trustees and C. R. Clauser, president of the Student Council, spoke on behalf of the student body.

Governor Leslie, along with four hundred faculty members, alumni, townspeople, and friends of the university were guests at a banquet held in the ballroom of the Memorial Union. The big event of the evening was not, as might be expected, the main address (or the telegram from President Herbert Hoover); it was the unveiling of the portrait of President Elliott by James W. Noel, an Indianapolis attorney and board member who presented the painting to the university on behalf of the trustees. The artist, Robert W. Grafton, was a prominent Michigan City painter who had received many similar commissions during those years. The painting now hangs in the foyer of the Edward C. Elliott Hall of Music.

It was a great moment for Elliott, one which afforded him great pleasure throughout his life. "The personal tribute of tonight has given to Mrs. Elliott and to me a new treasure for life's storehouse of precious moments," he said. "After all, what of greater value do we gather through the years than such memories?"

Reviewing his association with Purdue, Elliott said, "Your Purdue has had the best ten years of my life." He noted that nearly one-half of the value of the properties of Purdue had been added during these past ten years; one-half of the 12,000 alumni had received diplomas from him; and fully half of the students who had entered Purdue had entered since 1922. "My best ten years are not, by any measure, the best ten years of Purdue. The true happiness," he said, "is not in the past, nor in the present. The glory of Purdue is in the certainty and the power of its productive future." Using his highly favored alliterative phraseology, he said of his first decade at Purdue, "they have been years filled with adventure—adventures in dreaming and doing; in success and in failure; in prosperity and poverty; in drudgery and in delight; in responsibility and in helplessness; adventures with foes and with friends."

During the months that followed the Founder's Day affair, many articles appeared in various publications lauding Elliott and Purdue. David Ross observed that Elliott "knows and speaks the language of all groups, and is able to apply to their problems the sound judgment and wisdom borne from years of experience." Fritz Ernst, a Purdue grad, said "the alumni think he's a peach. He is very democratic, is a most able educator, and treats the students and alumni like real human beings."

Some time later the editor of the *Purdue Alumnus* contacted a few of Elliott's friends in the educational world for comments; Henry Suzzalo agreeably responded, ". . . there are few men in the U. S. who rank with President Elliott in his ability to contribute to every phase of public educational administration from policy making, government and organization to financial management and administrative execution. He is one of the outstanding University executives of the whole country." Suzzalo noted that Elliott had that ". . . high capacity for enlisting the enthusiastic cooperation of all the human factors which constitute an institution."

Another writer in the *Purdue Alumnus* described Elliott as having a "medium wiry physique, sharply chiseled features, deeply grooved character lines in his face, piercing eyes, and glossy brown hair. He walks a great deal, his gait is firm and quick. He enjoys smoking and talking with people." Virtually all writers, in one way or another, called attention to his "dynamic energy and tireless working." Some persons referred to him then (and many refer to him now) as a "tall" man, impressed with his erect carriage.

Actually he was perhaps 5′ 10″ or a little more, but he appeared to be "tall" and his bearing and manner were those of a tall man.

T. R. Johnston described him as "an immense talker" and "an excellent speaker." Using Elliott's own words, Johnston said that his audiences rightfully expected him to be "dignified without being dull, serious but not solemn, forceful yet not fanciful, truthful without too much triteness; to flavor his wisdom with dashes of wit; and to be peppy but not peppery." Appearing frequently before luncheon and dinner groups as a popular speaker, his favorite stance was at the side of the lectern, both hands plunged deep in his coat pockets, leaning slightly forward, alert, his eyes roving the group making many personal contacts. He demanded attentiveness, and he got it; Elliott loved to speak, and his audiences invariably acclaimed him.

It probably is both fair and accurate to say that Elliott's first decade at Purdue was his greatest. He had succeeded in bringing all elements of the university together to feel the new, enthusiastic, unified "spirit of Purdue."

Among his professional colleagues on the staff perhaps one in twenty was something less than in complete agreement with his methods; among the students at Purdue, perhaps one in two hundred viewed him as something other than a friend of students; while among the citizenry of the state, perhaps only one in two thousand felt something other than respect and admiration for the president.

As Elliott looked back at his ten years at Purdue, he probably also paused with Mrs. Elliott to look at the children's progress. Their youngest son, Ed, who had graduated from Jefferson High School in Lafayette that same spring (1932), was set to enter Purdue in the fall; John, who had never really considered going to Purdue, had graduated from Harvard University three years earlier; Susanne would be a senior at Vassar College the following fall; and Marion had completed her freshman year at Smith College.

They all had had good years at home with "Granny" and their mother and a very busy father. They enjoyed the warmth and depth of devotion that existed between their parents and loved to hear stories about Dad's problems. He occasionally regaled them with accounts of indignities suffered: the time as a student in Germany, for example, when he backed away from a painting in a museum to get a better view and fell over a balcony railing; though not seriously injured, he was highly indignant when the authorities arrested him for *trespassing* on the lawn below. On another occasion, while attending a sports dinner, he kept inching his chair backward as he listened to the other speakers until suddenly, to the great consternation and embarrassment of everyone, he and the chair toppled from the platform. To relieve everyone's concern he quipped, "That was the Notre Dame shift!" and the tension dissolved in laughter.

While at home they all had delighted to hear countless exchanges between mother and dad. Marion particularly treasured her father's propensity for coining "new" words as in the phrase, "her Elliottic mood." Mrs. Elliott would say, "There's no such word, Ned!" using her nickname for the president; but he would reply with conviction, "There is *now*, my dear!"

The children were pleased when the Elliotts entertained student leaders in their home as they frequently did. Elliott's relationships with students were cordial and always appropriate; his manner toward students was warm and friendly so that he and Mrs. Elliott were rather frequent guests at student affairs until his last years in office, the war years.

His relationships with the faculty during those first ten years and the years that followed were generally excellent, although there were those who fiercely opposed some of his actions and thought of him as a "taskmaster," a "dictator." His approach to faculty members and to faculty matters was largely individual and personal; and staff members responded as individuals. As one colleague confided, "You either loved him or you hated him," but there was always respect for his tremendous abilities and those who "loved" him far out-numbered the others.

Elliott could greet most faculty members by name and usually knew something of the personal background of each. For a time he attempted to have breakfast with every new job applicant and his wife. He boasted that he would never employ a staff member who didn't eat a hearty breakfast; and he wanted to see that the candidate had a healthy wife—one who wouldn't interfere with the man's work. At the same time he was urging the board to provide for higher faculty salaries proclaiming, "Why shouldn't we pay the instructors well? They do the work, don't they?"

He enjoyed his contacts with the staff and occasionally played golf with a foursome which included Professors G. A. Young, head of mechanical engineering; J. L. Cattel, head of modern languages; W. K. Hatt, head of civil engineering; and Jack E. Walters, director of personnel, Schools of Engineering.

Although he was not an accomplished golfer, he was good-natured about his golf scores and proclaimed himself a "duffer." Never an ardent participant in outdoor sports other than walking, Elliott had sometimes played golf at the Maple Bluff course in Madison, but gave up the game while in Montana.

In that state the most common sports activity was trout fishing and Elliott had enjoyed trips to the Bitterroot and Madison rivers. He and John occasionally went on Saturday fishing expeditions and, from time to time, he went on fishing trips with friends up in the mountains. In Indiana there was no trout fishing, of course, so Elliott renewed his golf game, partly for the exercise, perhaps more for the camaraderie.

His relationships with members of the board of trustees and various state and local officials were highly favorable and, again, were dependent to a large degree on his own personal magnetism. There was warm friendship and mutual respect and admiration between Elliott and board members Ross, Noel, Oliver, Marshall, Lilly, Hillenbrand, and Meredith; the same was true with Governor Leslie, and later with Governors Paul V. McNutt, Clifford M. Townsend, Henry F. Schricker, and many other state officials, legislators, and political leaders.

While it was sometimes said that Elliott was an opportunist in many if not all respects, his purposes always related to "the glory of old Purdue." When some of the "glory" spilled over to Elliott, he accepted it.

His frequent trips to visit alumni groups particularly during the first ten years paid great dividends. The alumni association flourished as Elliott made an all-out effort to get the support of alumni groups and individuals. Whereas his predecessor, Stone, had been somewhat disinterested in the old grads and, in fact, had alienated some of them, Elliott sought out and made friends with George Ade, John McCutcheon, Lawrence Downs, Russell Gray and many others, some nationally prominent, some who were local Purdue boosters.

In the summer of 1932 following the splendid testimonial dinner, however, the problems which faced Elliott and the university as a result of the depression left little time for the review of records of achievement.

In February of that year, Elliott had written that even though it was not easy to determine the meaning of the nation-wide economic disturbances of the past two years, it seemed clear that Purdue would need to re-examine its purposes, its structures, and its performances. "It is not unreasonable to conclude that the day may not be far distant when the whole enterprise of higher education . . . may be brought to trial under new codes of economy and of social effectiveness."

Elliott noted that while the university had outwardly continued with its usual activities, apparently little affected by the confusion and depression that had dominated and deflated the affairs of the material world, inwardly, the institution was preparing to change some of its plans in the event of "lean" years. Two years later he wrote, "the years that are lean are here."

THE DEPRESSION YEARS

From 1932 to 1937 virtually every problem of the university was related to finance and there were no ready solutions to most of them. Many have noted that Elliott was particularly alert to the opportunities for federal support of education, however, and he, together with R. B. Stewart, were highly successful in obtaining funds from such agencies as the Public Works Administration, the Works Progress Administration, and the National Youth Administration. Some writers have indicated that Purdue probably obtained far more than what might have been considered its "fair share" of federal dollars. In 1940 Elliott reported that federal grants during the period 1933-1940 had totaled more than $3,750,000.

At any rate, the president's task during this period was quite different from the duties of the earlier decade and it seemed to Elliott that the period from 1932 through 1940 constituted a "second stage" in his tenure at Purdue. Having firmly established himself as a strong, vigorous leader and a "Purdue man," he was able to act with a unified support that no other president at Purdue had previously enjoyed.

It would appear that Elliott was eminently successful during both periods of the university's history, but it is equally clear that he enjoyed the first decade far more than the next eight years.

During the summer of 1932 a special session of the legislature was called by the governor. The special tax for the "educational improvement fund," passed in 1929, was amended to provide for a three-year moratorium; a 15 per cent reduction in the university's appropriation for operating expenditures was approved and the interest coming from university funds was diverted to the state sinking fund. Thus the total dollar reduction was nearly 30 per cent for the academic year 1932-33.

As a result of these actions the board of trustees met on August 26, 1932, and reduced staff salaries from 10 to 15 per cent, based on the amount of salary the staff member received. Elliott, along with virtually everyone else, had his salary reduced (to $12,750). The board also noted that the legislature had ruled that the trustees could not increase any salary or add any new staff members without the specific approval of the State Budget Committee.

After the close of the special session of the legislature but before the board of trustees could meet to act, Elliott's mother died on August 15, 1932, in North Platte, Nebraska, two days before her 83rd birthday. The president and Mrs. Elliott were at her bedside. In the next issue of the *Purdue Alumnus,* Elliott wrote "life is just one hard thing after another."

In September, 1932, Elliott called a meeting of the presidents, secretaries, and treasurers of all campus organizations including fraternities and sororities. Two hundred students attended the meeting in Fowler Hall where they were asked to begin to plan a new economic policy for Purdue students for the coming year.

In his talk to student leaders Elliott said, "the country is facing a crisis today such as it has not known since the Civil War. All such institutions as Purdue are in very critical situations at present, and it becomes our duty to safeguard those interests that are essential to the University." He pointed out that there was an increase in the number of students applying for deferment of registration fees and also an increase in the number of demands on the student loan fund. He urged students not to incur heavy debts to remain in school and to cut their expenses to a minimum while at the university. He reported that every member of the university community, students and staff alike, were carrying on their work "under a very critical eye."

The outside activities of staff members came under scrutiny, for example, when the board of trustees, in December 1933, reviewed the circumstances under which a member of the faculty could be permitted to augment his university salary by performing commercial testing services or consulting with private firms. From the discussions came approval of policies and procedures recommended by the executive committee of the faculty which allowed staff members to accept payment under certain conditions for engaging in consulting work and service testing.

Student enrollment dropped in 1932-1933 for the first time since Elliott had taken office, and the number of students continued to decrease the following year. Not only was there a decline in students but also in appropriation of public money; and other income sources—fees, sales, rent, research grants, athletics —also were decreasing.

The Department of Athletics, for example, under Director Kellogg had been in some financial troubles even with its winning teams since the late 1920's and an alumni contact committee had been established to get the alumni appraised of the problems. By November 1932, Elliott and the board were exasperated over the fact that, despite their many efforts to improve the situation, spending in the athletic department still exceeded the income. Kellogg's salary was reduced and he was given until August 1934, to balance the budget or be terminated. Six months later (May 1933) he resigned in the face of what he thought was an impossible situation. He was succeeded by head football coach Noble E. Kizer.

In an effort to adjust the instruction of students to meet the changing social and economic conditions, Elliott announced that he questioned whether the university should attempt to serve as a custodial institution for those young people who were unable to find jobs and stayed in school merely following the line of least resistance. It seems apparent that he felt that the limited resources of the university should be concentrated upon superior students, "students of growing abilities."

Early in 1933 after he had met with the Committee on Free Schooling at Higher Levels at the "Citizens Conference on the Crisis in Education" held in Washington, D. C., he noted (in *The Purdue Alumnus*) that a large proportion of trained personnel in the established professions and the leaders in industrial and social life had come from the higher institutions; and furthermore, echoing his own statement made many years earlier, the results of the scientific research carried on by these institutions had been of incalculable worth to the economic life of the nation. When viewed from these two standpoints alone, he wrote, "the general scheme of higher education of the country must be regarded as a principal, productive asset, the conservation and further development of which are matters of permanent concern for the state and the nation."

One month later the 1933 Indiana legislature made a single lump sum appropriation (for the first time in history) and again drastically cut university income. The 1932 special session of the legislature had reduced appropriations 14.9 per cent. The 1933 legislature cut another 6.6 per cent for a total reduction of 21.5

per cent of the 1931 appropriation. Thus, including the cut resulting from the elimination of the "educational improvement fund,"
the total reduction in cost to the state was 35.3 per cent, according
to Elliott's figures.

On top of this "bad news," only shortly after the 1933 legislative
session was concluded, Elliott suffered his second great personal
loss when his father died on March 21, 1933, (on his 59th wedding
anniversary) at the age of 84 years. After having spent more than
50 years of his life in North Platte, Fred Elliott had made many
friends. An editorial in the local paper headed, "Fred Elliott was
a Giant Among Men," noted that "he accepted a humble position
for himself and [yet] through hard work and saving" he had given
his children the opportunity to move to "positions of trust and
responsibility." While the many expressions of sympathy were
heartening, death was especially hard to accept; both parents had
died at times when Elliott was already depressed and deeply concerned over the future of the university. But his answer to personal grief was to turn to his work with perhaps greater determination. After his father's death, however, Elliott told some of
his intimate friends about two prized possessions which were linked
irrevocably to his parents: a gold-cased Elgin watch which they
had given him on his 21st birthday in 1895, and a second gold-
cased watch, a Howard, which they gave him on his 50th birthday in 1924. Long after retirement he carried the Howard with
pride and affection.

Speaking before a conference of administrative officers from
engineering colleges in 1934, Elliott indicated that the times simply dictated new efficiences. "What is taught, how it is taught,
how much is taught, and who does the teaching are old questions
that are to receive new answers," he said. He suggested that all
courses could be cut down by leaving out superficial and irrelevant
materials. Similarly, a number of nonessential and marginal expenses of the students, could probably be eliminated by careful
planning, he observed.

Then there were other ways of being practically helpful to
another group, the unemployed graduates. He suggested that
superior students be encouraged and assisted toward graduate
study while others could be assigned to "scientific busy-work
projects."

Later that year (1934) a study was initiated by his office which
proposed to obtain information about the occupational standards
of Purdue graduates during the past five years. The work of the

study was done under the direction of Elliott by Frank C. Hockema, newly appointed assistant to the president, and Jack E. Walters.

When this study of occupational standards was published in 1935, there was evidence that of the group of 2,140 graduates from the classes of 1928-1934 who were questioned, more than 90 per cent were employed. And more than two-thirds of those gainfully employed were engaged in activities for which they were specifically trained by the university.

The following year Elliott and Hockema prepared a second report on Purdue graduates entitled *Where They Go and What They Do*. The reports of these studies were especially timely and undoubtedly served the purpose of creating new confidence in the worth of Purdue among the people of Indiana.

Hockema, a professor of industrial engineering, had been moved to his new position when a reorganization of the president's office was occasioned by the retirement of Helen Hand in September 1934. Miss Hand had served as secretary to the president of Purdue since 1913 and her leaving required that new assignments be made; she did continue on a part-time basis, however, working on special projects until her death in 1942. She had been of tremendous help to the president and had been accorded access to confidential matters as no others had.

The questionnaire used in the study mentioned above had asked that each graduate list the three best teachers he had had at Purdue and the three worst, together with reasons for his choice. The answers to these questions were known only to the president and Miss Hand.

Elliott told the faculty what he had done, emphasizing the confidential nature of the results, but he was pleased when several professors were anxious to know how they rated.

Reminiscing, Elliott recalled twenty years later that most of those who came to see him were the best ones; he assumed that the poorer teachers probably didn't care. Elliott told of one young man who felt that he had probably received a lot of criticism and came to see if his suspicions were correct. The file of responses revealed the professor had been attacked severely. He told Elliott that he would resign immediately, but the president advised him to wait until tomorrow before making a final decision.

The next morning the man appeared for another talk and finally was persuaded to stay and work to become a better teacher; the president promised to help. With a great deal of satisfaction

Elliott recalled that the professor had remained at Purdue and eventually received an award for outstanding teaching.

Another case involved a professor in engineering who first came to Elliott's attention at one of his meetings with the members of Iron Key on a Sunday morning. The boys complained that the man was sarcastic, ridiculed students, called them incompetent, and so forth. When Elliott confirmed these comments from the questionnaire, he saw the department head, advised him to call in the professor, talk it over, and give him every possible assistance to help him become more effective. The head later reported that the individual had become one of the best teachers in the department.

Elliott insistently urged deans and department heads to work with teachers, supervising, stimulating and helping them to do their best work. At times he pushed for better teaching until he irritated some members of the faculty. "Some of the men on this faculty are noted for never seeing a student," he would exclaim bitterly; and it sometimes seemed as though he would much perfer to support a student rather than any faculty member in a conflict between the two. Part of his constant drive for better teaching undoubtedly came from his background in professional education, part of it from his genuine interest in student progress, but part of it came from his interest in getting the best out of each individual, student and teacher alike.

Hockema had a reputation as an excellent teacher, was vitally interested in student welfare, and eventually became (with R. B. Stewart) one of the two-man administrative team closest to Elliott.

Elliott's review of the 61st year of the university (1934-1935) made little mention of the effect of the depression, but did list several events which Elliott thought gave "a certain distinction to the year." He mentioned the opening of the new women's residence hall in September 1934, made possible by a grant from the federal Public Works Administration, which provided for the first time "proper housing facilities for 120 women students of the University."

He noted also the granting of direct aid to students by the federal Emergency Relief Administration; the Homes Conference already referred to; the preparation of plans for a new Student Service and Administration Building (later named the Executive Building); and the appointment to the staff of Dr. Lillian M. Gilbreth as professor of industrial engineering, and Miss Amelia Earhart as consultant on careers for women. "These appointments," he said, "were made with the intention of introducing new forces for the study of one of the most important modern unsolved problems of higher education—the effective education of young women."

Elliott had for some time been interested in the education of college women. He first saw Miss Earhart at a conference in New York City sponsored by the New York *Herald Tribune* in September 1934. Elliott was on the program of the Fourth Annual Women's Conference on Current Problems to speak on "New Frontiers for Youth." Amelia Earhart followed him on the program, speaking on the future of aeronautics and the part women were to play in the development of that field. She had just completed her notable flight over the Atlantic and her comments were of great interest to Elliott.

That evening Elliott began to mull over the possibilities that could come about if Amelia Earhart and Purdue University could be related in some way. The next day at a luncheon arranged by Elliott, he, Miss Earhart, and her husband, George Palmer Putnam, discussed some possibilities. Elliott later reported that it was at this time that he learned that "her primary interest in life was not in this career of adventure upon which she had embarked, but rather in an effort to find and make some additions to the solution to the problem of careers for women." She was interested primarily in the education of women in order to qualify them for their place in the world, Elliott observed. He asked her to come to the campus and state her philosophy; she was delighted at the prospect. Within an hour after the luncheon was over, Elliott had made several phone calls, Miss Earhart had rearranged her schedule, and in less than a month Miss Earhart was on the Purdue campus to address faculty members and women students on "Opportunities For Women In Aviation." She was the guest of three coed activities, the Women's Self-Governing Association, the Young Women's Christian Association, and the Women's Athletic Association. It was the first of a series of visits to the campus, the last of which was to precede her ill-fated flight in the Purdue "Flying Laboratory," in 1937.

In the spring of 1935, Miss Earhart returned to campus to visit with the Elliott family. President and Mrs. Elliott met her in Fort Wayne on March 22, and she returned to Lafayette with them to discuss what kind of arrangements could be made in order for her to become affiliated with the university. Two and a half months later, the president announced the appointment of Miss Earhart as a visiting member of the faculty. Well aware of her popularity, Elliott said, "Miss Earhart represents better than any other young woman of this generation the spirit and the courageous skill which may be called the new pioneering." The following November she took up her duties at the university as consultant on careers for women.

Although she was never on the campus at any one time for more than a few weeks, the days spent at Purdue were busy ones. While on campus for her intermittent visits, she generally stayed in one of the women's residence halls. According to Putnam, her husband and biographer, Miss Earhart never became quite reconciled to her high-sounding title, but he wrote that "even in the fortuitously shortened period in it she found her job at Purdue University one of the most satisfying adventures in her life." Both Elliott and Putnam agreed that although the relationship came about quite by chance, it almost seemed foreordained.

Putnam reported that President Elliott asked him what he thought most interested Miss Earhart in the field of research and education beyond immediate academic matters.[7] Putnam said he told Elliott that she was "hankering for a bigger and better plane, not only one in which she could go to far places farther and faster and more safely, but to use as a laboratory for research in aviation education and for technical experimentation."

Miss Earhart discussed these possibilities with Elliott, Ross, and others, and there was established in the Purdue Research Foundation an Amelia Earhart Fund for Aeronautical Research. Elliott announced that the fund had been established in April, 1936, and that $50,000 had been subscribed. Chief contributors to the fund were David Ross, J. K. Lilly, Vincent Bendix, and others, mostly within the aviation industry. From this growing fund was purchased the $80,000 Lockheed Electra which became known as the Purdue "Flying Laboratory." After a number of test flights Miss Earhart brought the "Flying Laboratory" to the Purdue University Airport and to other major cities over the country getting various pieces of equipment and support for her projected round-the-world flight. Her last official visit to the university as a coed counselor was in November 1936.

The story of her flight and the tragic end of her career has been told many times. The most notable of these are Putnam's book, *Soaring Wings;* Muriel Earhart Morrissey's *Courage Is The Price;* Paul L. Briand's *Daughter of the Sky;* and Fred Goerner's

The Search for Amelia Earhart. It was later pointed out that the day that the last radio contact was made with her, July 2, 1937, was the day she was to have appeared at Purdue University to speak on "What Next In The Air." On the 16th of July, 1937, when apparently all hope had gone, Elliott wired her husband saying, "George, she would not want us to grieve or weep; she would have been a heroine in any age."

Putnam was undeniably impressed with Elliott even though their association was an occasional one, extending over only a few years. He loved to mingle with celebrities (and near-celebrities) and was especially delighted with opportunities for stimulating conversation. Elliott, of course, was always happy when engaged in good conversation and privately deplored those dinner guests who "only opened their mouths to put food in." Several years after his visits to Purdue Putnam wrote:

> Each year we see lists of the ten best-dressed women, the best-dressed men, the best books, the best plays. Any literate child with a respectable I. Q. knows the standing of Mrs. Harrison Williams and Lucius Beebe. But something ought to be done about those who carry the torch of conversation. My own nominations would include such gracious performers as Leopold Stokowski, Frank Crowninshield, Clare Boothe, Clifton Fadiman, Missy Meloney, President Elliott of Purdue, Helen Reid, Hendrik Willem Van Loon, Gilbert Adrian, and, of course, Royal Cortissoz.[8]

In the spring of 1939, Putnam presented a full-length portrait of Amelia Earhart to Purdue University; Elliott accepted the oil painting for the university to hang in the residence hall where Miss Earhart stayed during her visits to the campus.

Whether her use of the "Flying Laboratory" provided for any significant research in aviation education and/or technical experimentation is a matter for conjecture. There certainly are those who feel that the Purdue Research Foundation squandered literally thousands of dollars without any substantial return. From Elliott's view, the association was a rewarding one upon which no dollar value could ever be placed. The loss of Amelia Earhart was the nation's loss, but the legend of Amelia Earhart is a part of the history of Purdue University. While Elliott and everyone else associated with the project had hoped for more, the tragic conclusion was to Elliott another example of the fate that had brought the two together. In December 1937, Elliott went to New York City and presented the maps, log book notes, weather reports, and other data gathered by Miss Earhart to the World Center of Women's Archives. Many other materials relating to Amelia Earhart are in the Purdue University library.

The appointment of Dr. Lillian M. Gilbreth was announced within a short time after Amelia Earhart had accepted her counseling position. Mrs. Gilbreth, famed industrial engineer, author, and widowed mother of twelve children (*Cheaper by the Dozen*), joined the staff as a professor of industrial engineering in the General Engineering Department (effective September 1935) with the understanding that she would spend four or five two-week periods on campus each year to lecture and consult with students in engineering.

Mrs. Gilbreth maintained her home in Montclair, New Jersey, and continued her consulting work across the nation, but while on campus she stayed in the Women's Residence Hall where she could readily talk with coeds. She later extended her areas of interest at Purdue to include work with students and faculty members in the Schools of Home Economics and Agriculture, studying the place of management in the home and on the farm.

Certainly as well known among engineers as Miss Earhart, Mrs. Gilbreth became a familiar and charming figure on campus, greatly admired by all who came in contact with her. Forever linked with Purdue in the minds of her students, Mrs. Gilbreth later gave to the university the Gilbreth Engineering Library of about 1500 volumes plus many original notes relating to studies in time and motion and fatigue which she and her husband, Frank Gilbreth, made during his lifetime. Named a consultant in careers for women after Miss Earhart's death, Mrs. Gilbreth's appointment was further indication of Elliott's interest in and concern for the education of women in the university; she continued her official connection with Purdue until her retirement in 1948, and has been an occasional visitor since that time.

OUT OF THE DEPRESSION

In a report published to coincide with the opening of the 1937 legislative session, Elliott reported that the appropriation for resident teaching in 1935-1936 had been $1,185,000, an increase of only 12.8 per cent over that appropriated for the 1925-1926 school year. During the same ten-year period the net annual enrollment of students had risen nearly 45 per cent. He reported that unless more dollars were provided for instructional space, for the replacement of supplies, for the rehabilitation of obsolete equipment, for the acquisition of new machinery and equipment, and for the restoration of the salary reductions made in 1933, the chances of the university maintaining its high place among the technical institutions of the country were indeed small.

The 1937 legislature, influenced to a degree at least by Elliott's review of the situation, provided funds which permitted a general restoration of salaries to the 1932 levels and the board promptly voted to restore Elliott's salary to the $15,000 level where it was to remain until his retirement.

Of greater importance to Elliott, however, was the legislative appropriation of $50,000 for the purpose of establishing a retirement program for faculty and staff. On the recommendation of Elliott and R. B. Stewart, the board immediately voted to complete arrangements with the Teachers Insurance and Annuity Association (an agency established by the Carnegie Foundation for the Advancement of Teaching) to provide retirement allowances for the university staff. The action was one of the major achievements of his administration and perhaps symbolized the end of the depression for the university.

The legislature also voted to reinstate the mill tax, suspended in 1932, to become effective July 1, 1937. Payments were to begin July 1, 1938. The 1939 legislature eliminated the mill tax, however, and this type of tax levy was never used again during Elliott's presidency to make dollars available for higher education.

In his review of the academic year 1936-1937, Elliott prepared a summary of federal grants and expenditures at Purdue that had been made by the federal government since 1933 in an effort to meet the national economic emergency. The Public Works Administration had expended more than $700,000 toward the construction of five new buildings: two units of the women's residence halls, the Executive Building, a field house and gymnasium for men, and an addition to the Purdue Memorial Union Building. Through the Works Progress Administration more than $413,000 had been spent for an airport hangar, an addition to the Physics Building, tennis courts, roadways, sewers, fences, and sundry campus improvements. And the National Youth Administration had paid almost $202,000 to needy students for work done in various departments of the university.

In later years, Elliott remarked that in the beginning of the National Youth Administration, he was not in favor of the plan to provide student aid. He felt that greater emphasis should have been placed upon aid to students of superior ability instead of basing that aid upon economic circumstances. After nine years of experience with that type of financial help, Elliott said, however, that the NYA had exerted a "most beneficial effect upon our youth, not merely by providing needed financial assistance, . . . but also by maintaining their morale."

During the summer of 1938 the Board of Regents of the University of the Philippines sent one of their members, Manuel A. Roxas (who later became president of the Republic), to the United States to select two leading educators to serve as educational advisors to the Committee on Educational Policy. The board was in the process of reorganizing the administration and instruction of the university.

Roxas, chairman of the committee, talked with Paul Monroe at Teachers College who had made a school study in the Philippines in 1915; with Samuel P. Capen, chancellor of the University of Buffalo; with Lotus D. Coffman, president of the University of Minnesota; and a number of others, including Elliott.

Elliott's name was undoubtedly high on the list partly because of the efforts of Paul V. McNutt, United States Commissioner to the Philippines and former governor of Indiana (1933-37), and partly because of Elliott's reputation as a member of numerous survey teams.

Elliott was reluctant to make the trip he said, until Roxas offered to pay Mrs. Elliott's expenses in order to get her to come along. With that added inducement, he discussed the matter with the board and received approval to take a leave of absence for the first semester of the 1938-39 school year. It was agreed that an administrative committee consisting of Frank C. Hockema; R. B. Stewart; Dean A. A. Potter; and H. J. Reed, acting director of the Agricultural Experiment Station; would handle the affairs of the university.

So on September 12, 1938, the president and Mrs. Elliott left Lafayette to begin their first and only long vacation trip together. Shortly after their steamship, *Empress of Canada,* docked in the harbor at Manila on October 9, they joined Paul C. Packer, dean of the College of Education at the University of Iowa, who had been selected by Roxas as the second advisor.

During their stay in the Philippines, Packer and Elliott visited every college, school, and unit of the University, interviewing deans and other administrative officials, faculty members, and student leaders. The advisors were pressed for time in which to prepare a series of twenty-seven memoranda and discuss each of these with the committee. A final meeting was held on December 20, 1938, at which time Elliott made an oral summary of the advisors' findings before the board of regents and the President of the Philippines, Manuel L. Quezon. Five days later on Christmas Day, the Elliotts left Manila to return to the United States.

The trip home was a delightful vacation for the Elliotts. They went from Manila to Naples, visited the Riviera and Paris, traveled to England where he visited Ramsgate for the third time, then sailed for home on the maiden westward voyage of the *Queen Mary*. Arriving in New York on February 10, 1939, Elliott addressed the Purdue Alumni Club of New York City that night. They returned to Lafayette on Sunday, February 12, and were guests at a dinner party given by the Purdue Women's Club the next evening. The events immediately following his return to New York made it abundantly clear that he was back as president of Purdue.

Many "welcome home" dinners were given, but the largest was sponsored by the University Club, when on February 20, 1939, about 600 persons attended a dinner-dance in the Purdue Memorial Union Ballroom. In attendance were eight Indiana college presidents; Herman B Wells of Indiana University, the Reverend John F. O'Hara of Notre Dame, and L. B. Hopkins of Wabash College, among others, were called on to welcome the Elliotts back to Lafayette.

Purdue's greatest period of building during Elliott's presidency began in 1929 and lasted through the depression to 1940. A total of twelve major buildings were constructed plus extensive additions to a number of other buildings. In his report for 1938-1939, Elliott included a table presenting an analysis of the increase in the physical facilities of the university during the decade 1929-1939. "The records show," he wrote, "that the value of the building assets in 1929 was somewhat less than $4\frac{1}{2}$ million. During the decade . . . these assets have been tripled in value."

His review of the next year was devoted to a discussion of "needs yet to be met" on the Purdue campus. Elliott wrote that fifteen years ago he had stated that not less than $10,000,000 was required for the improvement and extension of the physical plant. During the intervening years more than $10,000,000 had been spent for the construction and equipment of buildings on the campus, but even this amount had not matched the needs of the institution.

He concluded that not less than $5,000,000 was yet needed to provide facilities for the work of the university. He went ahead to itemize the needs carefully under twenty headings. At the end of the next year he was able to announce that contracts had been let for the construction of the final unit of the Electrical Engineering Building and the Duncan High Tension Laboratory, the Physics Building, and a transmitting station for radio station WBAA. Virtually all major construction stopped after these buildings were completed, however, because of the national defense effort.

Reviewing more than the building program at Purdue during Elliott's term, T. R. Johnston and Helen Hand wrote in *The Archives of Purdue* in 1940:

> Under his dynamic leadership, Purdue has made its greatest progress, far surpassing the development during all of the other regimes. Under his leadership the value of the physical plant has more than quadrupled, . . . many buildings have gone up not only for classroom work but also for living quarters for students and for athletic and other recreational activities. . . . Enrollment has gone from 3,110 to 7,121. . . . The number of people coming . . . for short courses and conferences has risen from three or four thousand a year to well above 40,000. The research program has been expanded greatly. . . . The relationship with the public has been greatly strengthened. . . .9

At 65 years of age, Elliott was still vigorously espousing the work of Purdue University and higher education generally. "During the year (1940)," he noted in the annual report, "I find that I attended and spoke at seventy dinners—fifty of these on campus and twenty in other parts of the state and country; I also spoke at fifty other meetings." Even though he had made what he called an "earnest effort" to cut down on the number of speaking engagements, it still seemed necessary for him to continue strengthening the "relationship with the public" by making personal appearances.

Elliott was a well-known and popular figure in Indiana in 1940 and many people were not particularly surprised when early that year an Associated Press story announced that Frank M. McHale, Democratic party national committeeman and director of Paul V. McNutt's campaign for the presidential nomination, was spearheading a movement to get Elliott to become a candidate for the Democratic Party nomination for governor of Indiana.

The preceding June (1939), McNutt had returned from his post as United States Commissioner to the Philippines and Elliott had been chosen to make the major address at the homecoming celebration in Indianapolis. After he had been named as the official "welcomer," some people wondered if he were being groomed as a gubernatorial candidate.

Within a few days after the story was released, however, Elliott issued a statement to the local newspaper which said in part, "I have never been and am not now a candidate for any political office whatever." Alluding to other items concerning his possible candidacy that had appeared in the newspapers following the AP release Elliott wrote, "I hope that there will be no further effort to divert me from the educational things I know how to do, to the political things for which I am not adapted."

Evidently he also contacted McHale and others in the party for there were no other overt attempts to get Elliott into the political arena until several years later.

Almost a year after his retirement, however, when Elliott was seventy-one years old, several newspapers in the state reported that a number of "leading Democrats in the state" had asked him to become a candidate for the Democratic Party nomination to the United States Senate. Again Elliott declined to enter the race saying, "It is my conclusion that I do not possess the personal or political qualifications for seeking or serving in the office, therefore, I ask that my name not be used."

Although there may have been some individuals who felt that Elliott would have liked to hold a political office, there is no evidence that he was even willing to consider for more than a moment the possibility of a political career.

Virtually every citizen of the state felt it was appropriate when Indiana University, celebrating the 120th anniversary of its founding, awarded Elliott his sixth honorary degree on May 2, 1940. He had received degrees from Oregon Agricultural College in 1930 and from the University of Nebraska in 1936 in addition to those previously mentioned; and in later years he was similarly honored by Hahneman Medical College and Hospital (1941), University of Pittsburgh (1943), Illinois Institute of Technology (1944), Purdue University (1946), and Temple University (1949). Although he said that there were "too many synthetic doctors pluming themselves in the academic world," he was, nevertheless, highly pleased when he was selected to receive an honorary degree. Especially gratifying were those from Columbia, Nebraska, Indiana, and Purdue.

Two days after the ceremonial at Indiana University, Elliott presided at another celebration, the opening of Purdue's new Hall of Music, billed as the largest theatre in the world at that time. It was a grand occasion, a climax to the building program, and Elliott was delighted to add this dedication ceremony "to the many hours of triumph already possessed by Purdue." As R. B. Stewart later recounted, Elliott had "almost single-handedly obtained the federal aid, asked and received a state appropriation, and planned the bond issue to assure construction costs," and he was justifiably proud of the result.

Without knowing that the great auditorium would be called the Edward C. Elliott Hall of Music by future generations, he said, "This Hall of Music, by whatever name it may later be known, is not (solely) a means for diversion. . . ." Speaking at the Gala Week ceremony he said, "Here through the years, unnumbered men, women, and children will come to see, to listen, to think, and thus be made over and higher, little by little, through their seeing and hearing and thinking."

Always interested in student life and student activities, Elliott had been a great fan and an ardent booster of Purdue athletics. During the late twenties and early thirties he had followed Purdue's championship teams in both football and basketball, particularly pleased when their youngest son, Ed, played on three championship basketball teams from 1933-34 through 1935-36 under Coach Ward "Piggy" Lambert. And in 1935 he had established an annual award, "The Elliott Plaque," which was to go to the student residing in Cary Hall who had been most outstanding in intercollegiate athletics. A medal has been presented to each winner and his name has been attached to the plaque which today hangs in Cary Hall.

But in 1940 he involved himself more deeply in athletic affairs than he had ever envisioned possible. Athletic director and head football coach Noble E. Kizer died in June of that year and Elliott was forced to take over as athletic director for several months, naming Allen "Mal" Elward as head football coach and assistant athletic director. Ed felt that his dad enjoyed that particular assignment more than he had expected. He visited regularly with the coaches and football players, stopping by the field almost every evening on his way home. He ate at the training table on a number of occasions and seemed to develop a special bond with the athletes and members of the athletic staff during that period.

When questioned by a reporter regarding the news that the University of Chicago had dropped out of Big Ten football, Elliott remarked that the action was "courageous and significant" and told the sports writer that it was "within the range of possibilities that the University of Chicago will demonstrate the possibility of conducting a university without football." In the same interview he said, "There have been times that I have wished that we might have colleges and universities without football. This perhaps is a bit too Utopian. Perhaps Chicago will prove that Utopia is possible. But Purdue is not Utopia and intends to continue to play football—and, we hope, good football."

In January 1941 he gave up the post, naming Elward athletic director; the athletic department promptly awarded him a "P" sweater with a star (normally given to the captain of the team) which he accepted and treasured as the years went by.

At the close of the year 1940-1941, it was clear, however, that Elliott and the university were to become more and more concerned with the effect of the National Defense Program on the university. During that year, 33 staff members had withdrawn from the university in order to participate in the National Defense Program, and leaves of absence had been granted to those staff members called to military duty. By the end of the following year, of course, the university had changed from "a defense footing to a war footing." The "second stage" of his Purdue years was over.

THE WAR YEARS

The attack on Pearl Harbor, December 7, 1941, had its immediate effect on Purdue University and similar institutions all over the nation. One of the first acts of the president of the university was to call a special student convocation for December 15, 1941, in the new Hall of Music. The day was set aside as "Bill of Rights Day," and Elliott talked to the student body regarding the individual's part in the war effort. Intimating that the student's place was in the classroom as he had indicated twenty-five years earlier in Montana during World War I, he presented a list of duties which he called a "Bill of Responsibilities" for Purdue students. "You have the responsibility," he said, "for reducing social activities, for rigid economy in your personal affairs, and for maintaining your health and physical fitness." He predicted that the university would make a rapid change to a war-time basis.

Within three weeks after the declaration of war the executive committee of the faculty determined that for the duration of the war, the university would operate on an accelerated teaching schedule of three sixteen-week terms a year, eliminating final exams and vacation periods. When Elliott reported later on the activities of the year 1941-1942, he noted briefly that the university had begun to secure the maxium utilization of all its resources for war purposes. These were times that demanded an organized concentration of effort. By the end of the year he could only write that any report of progress would be sketchy and incomplete.

In January 1942, it was announced that Elliott had been named to serve on a Committee on War-Time Requirements for Specialized Personnel, a subcommittee of the National Resources Planning Board. Six months earlier he had turned down a request from Edward Stettinius to serve as a consultant to the office of production management.

At a second special student convocation in February 1942, he suggested that students remember that while they were not all in uniform or in a training camp in reality, they were at the "Purdue training center" where "the primary business is to prepare you for some meaningful job of the war." Elliott had firm convictions as to how the college student fitted into the war effort.

He believed in the fundamental principle of selective service, the assignment of every man and woman "according to ability to every job according to its need." To him this meant that practically all able-bodied and able-minded male students should be directed to the armed forces but that those who were not physically fit for combat should be trained "for scarcity fields of need." "This is total war," he wrote, "requiring all of our power of material and men."

Then, early in 1942, newly appointed War Manpower Commissioner, Paul V. McNutt, asked Elliott to become Chief of the Division of Professional and Technical Employment and Training within the War Manpower Commission. Elliott was eager to accept the assignment. After considerable discussion the board approved his request for a leave of absence and Elliott left for Washington on June 22, 1942, to take over his new job about July 1, 1942.

It was not known at that time how long he would be on leave, but the operation of the university was once again turned over to a committee of Hockema, Stewart, Potter, and Reed (who had

Dr. Lillian M. Gilbreth talked with Elliott in his office in April 1935.

The first honorary degrees awarded by Purdue were presented in June 1926 to four distinguished alumni. Pictured on that occasion were (left to right): Chase S. Osborn, Dean Stanley Coulter, John T. McCutcheon, C. H. Robertson, George Ade, and President Elliott.

Mrs. Franklin D. Roosevelt and Indiana Governor Paul V. McNutt looked at one of the Better Homes in America experimental houses in June 1936.

The cornerstone laying ceremonies for the Chemical Engineering Building were held on March 31, 1939.

Cornerstone ceremonies at the Edward C. Elliott Hall of Music were held August 31, 1939. Along with Elliott are (left to right) comptroller R. B. Stewart, board president David Ross, and architect Walter Scholer.

The stone reliefs at the entrance to the Purdue Memorial Union Building were dedicated November 3, 1939, during Homecoming Weekend. Pictured here (left to right) are Frances Rich, sculptress; her sister, Jane Rich; Elliott; and former screen star, Irene Rich, the artist's mother.

The president worked at his desk in the Executive Building, April 1940.

In May 1940 the Athletic Department presented Elliott with a "P" jacket with the captain's star. He had just completed a six month self-imposed assignment as athletic director.

In November 1940, Miss Jacqueline Cochrane came to Purdue to participate in a Women's Vocational Conference.

Indiana Governor Henry F. Schricker and David Ross talked with Elliott at a reception in the Claypool Hotel, Indianapolis, on May 27, 1942.

Elliott invariably plunged his hands in his coat pockets as he spoke at hundreds of banquets. Here he is addressing The Engineering Institute of Canada in Toronto in February 1943.

Tomato King Jack Stubblefield chatted with Elliott at the State Tomato Festival at Terre Haute in August 1943.

As president emeritus, Elliott was provided an office in the Executive Building for as long as he lived. In April 1949, he was photographed at his desk, an alert 74 years of age.

This sculpture (along with a bust of David E. Ross) was presented to the University by Allison E. Stewart, president of the board of trustees. Unveiled at the Homecoming Banquet on October 22, 1949, the work was done by Jon Johnson, Indiana sculptor, who also did much of the facade work on the Edward C. Elliott Hall of Music. Elliott and Mrs. Elliott were photographed with the bust immediately following the presentation.

When he was 80 years old, Elliott was serving as a consultant for the Army Ordnance Corps at Aberdeen Proving Ground, November 1955.

One of the last photographs of Elliott was taken at home on his 85th birthday, December 21, 1959, six months before his death.

"Here through the years, unnumbered men, women, and children will come to see, to listen, to think, and thus be made over and higher, little by little, through their seeing and hearing and thinking," said Elliott speaking at the 1940 dedication ceremonies for the Hall of Music, later named in his honor.

replaced Dean of Agriculture J. H. Skinner after his retirement in June 1939). It was the same group that had served in 1938 when Elliott was in the Philippines.

Unfortunately, only a few weeks after Elliott's departure, David Ross suffered a massive stroke and was immediately placed in a local hospital, completely incapable of carrying on any of his activities as president of the board. The administrative committee, severely handicapped by this unexpected circumstance, was forced to accept additional responsibilities and Elliott found that he could not divorce himself from the affairs of the university as completely as he had expected. Nevertheless, a committment had been made, and all the individuals involved were pledged to a total war effort—Elliott's commitment, however, was to the War Manpower Commission.

Within the division which Elliott directed were four sections: The National Roster, which maintained a classified record of the nation's scientific and specialized manpower; the Procurement and Assignment Service, which was charged with the allocation of the physicians, surgeons, dentists, and veterinarians for both civilian and armed forces needs; the Engineering Science and Management War Training, a program carried on by more than 200 higher schools; and the section on the Utilization of Colleges and Universities. His primary task was to define ways in which colleges and universities could assist in the war effort.

After having spent a little more than two months with the War Manpower Commission, Elliott suggested that there were at least four ways for colleges, universities, and professional and technical schools to assist the Army, Navy, and the commission in their training programs. He advocated using every available means for promoting the physical fitness of students; taking every effort to make each student feel that he was an active participant in the war effort, recognizing that each student had been detailed to an institution for some form of training required by either the Armed Forces, the war production industries, or some necessary public service; advising and encouraging all students sufficiently able-bodied to enlist; and by developing courses which would make every student "keenly conscious of the nature of the cause that the nation has been called to defend."

While testifying before the House of Representatives Committee on Military Affairs, Elliott spoke of a number of more specific ideas which he thought would further develop the nation's plan for providing professionally trained men for the armed forces.

The hearing was primarily concerned with the topic "lowering the draft age to eighteen years," but a number of general questions were asked and Elliott was led into other considerations. He observed that, "this is, above all, first a war of science and that nation that has the scientists with the ability to apply that science to the destructive arts of war and to self-protection is the nation that is best armed." He thought that the selection of those who were to be educated in the universities might well be left to the local draft boards, but that the advanced training in technical subjects should be done only in the institutions already staffed and equipped to do that work.

Elliott advocated a plan whereby all young men would be inducted to the service according to the Selective Service System, some detailed back to colleges and universities for training, and then some of those trained men could be returned to work in industry or civilian life. Elliott worked closely, of course, with Major General Lewis B. Hershey, director of the Selective Service System, and they served together on many committees.

Elliott's testimony indicated that he regarded military training as one of the essential parts of higher education in America. When pressed further, Elliott said that he had a "very pronounced prejudice in favor of military training" even for boys under age eighteen who were enrolled in secondary schools. During the next few years, he strongly urged that military training be included in the educational program, even to the extent of having universal military training.

In March 1943, he stated his belief firmly and succinctly, "If the nation is sensible in its foresight, adequate provision will be made for what has come to be called Universal Military Training of our youth." Still later (1945) he published an article in the *American Legion Magazine* that was largely devoted to a plea for universal military training. "More than fifty years ago I came under a system of compulsory military training," he recalled, "and since that long ago Autumn day when I served as a more or less unwilling member of the Cadet Battalion at the University of Nebraska, then under the command of Lt. John J. Pershing of the Tenth United States Cavalry, I have been a supporter of military training as an essential part of American civic education." On at least three other occasions following the war, Elliott strongly supported universal military training. It appears that his work with the War Manpower Commission merely strengthened a feeling which had been developing since his student days at the University of Nebraska.

A small group of students at Purdue had found out how he felt three years earlier when a peace organization requested permission to carry out a non-violent demonstration against the Selective Service and Training Act of 1940. They wanted to declare Wednesday, October 16, 1940, (Conscription Registration Day) a day of mourning and planned to wear black arm bands for the occasion. Elliott emphatically denied the organization "the privilege of carrying out this plan," and when the peace group attempted to schedule a public meeting that evening on campus, Elliott saw to it that that event was also cancelled. The board went on record as supporting his decisive stand.

After only four months in Washington, Elliott was impressed with the tremendously difficult task which confronted the nation's schools; the liberal arts colleges, for example, posed an intricate problem.

As Elliott pointed out in later years, "a definite place was easily found in the war training program for all professional schools, such as medicine, dentistry, engineering, etc., and also for various types of vocational schools on the secondary level." But, he continued, this was not so in the case of the liberal arts college. Although the leaders of the liberal arts colleges were eager to do their part in the war effort and be assigned a place in the war training program, not many were added to the program. Elliott had hoped, of course, that plans could be devised which would provide for the most effective utilization of *all* colleges and universities in the war effort.

The plans that he considered most effective were generally based on the Selective Service scheme, which was designed to pick specific people to work on specific jobs. At a second congressional committee hearing in February 1943, Representative John J. Sparkman pointed out that a great many people were afraid of such a program and referred to it as regimentation. Elliott agreed that such plans were likely to arouse opposition, but he felt that the national emergency demanded immediate action. "We have got to be prepared to give up a large amount of our individual liberty," he said, "in order that we may have some national liberty left after the job is done."

In the spring of 1943, the organization which he directed was operating the entire program involving the training of service men in higher institutions. The complete story of the effectiveness of the division is not available for study. But clearly there were many problems which had not been solved and some which would never be solved.[10] After nearly a year with the War Manpower Commission, however, Elliott apparently became convinced that he could not continue in that capacity and still carry on his work as president of Purdue University.

On the Purdue campus, even though Elliott had made numerous trips between Washington and Lafayette and had never missed a board meeting, many members of the faculty (and some board members) as well as some of the students felt that Elliott was sorely needed in Lafayette. So in April 1943, he resigned from the commission and returned to full-time duties in the Executive Building.

While Elliott was still readjusting to a university that was quite different from the institution that he had known so well ten months earlier, Purdue lost one of its greatest leaders, David Ross. Without question the death of Ross (on June 28, 1943), was a tremendous shock to Elliott and to the entire university community. He had been elected to the board of trustees the year before Elliott had come to Purdue and had been president of the board since 1927. He was certainly Elliott's closest friend at Purdue and probably his greatest supporter. George Ade referred to the two-man team as Damon and Pythias; and another staff member who had many opportunities to see them work together called Ross "both an apt student and a strong ally" of Elliott.

Ross, like Elliott, has been the subject of hundreds of Purdue-related stories, but his biographer, Fred C. Kelly, has written the only comprehensive life story. Unfortunately, Kelly did not acknowledge that Elliott exerted any considerable influence on Ross and from time to time implies that Elliott was valuable chiefly as an administrative advisor to Ross. It has appeared to most observers, however, that the Elliott-Ross team was just that— a most fortunate combination of talented individuals whose goals for Purdue were nearly identical, whose abilities were commensurate, and whose personalities were almost completely compatible.

For 15 years they had met together with regularity. When both Elliott and Ross were in town they met almost daily, frequently at Ross's office where Elliott stopped on his way to the university, or at Elliott's home in the evening. Even though Ross had been lost as an effective board member for nearly a year, it was not until his death that Elliott received the full impact of the loss. "This is a sorrowful day for Purdue University," he mourned.

The shock to the university was intensified as a result of two other deaths, Dean Emeritus Stanley Coulter and Professor G. A. Young; all three men were Purdue legends—all died within a three-day period.

Almost immediately, the trustees selected long-time board member James W. Noel to replace Ross as president of the board, and at the request of Elliott, they named Hockema to a new post of executive dean where he quickly assumed additional responsibilities in the President's Office. Noel, however, was destined to serve in that capacity for less than a year; he died in April 1944, and John A. Hillenbrand was elected board president.

Within a few weeks Purdue lost still another strong booster with the passing of George Ade on May 16, 1944. Because he had been so attached to Purdue and to Elliott, members of the family asked Elliott to join two other of Ade's good friends, John T. McCutcheon and Judge Kenesaw Mountain Landis, at the funeral where the three men talked informally about Ade as a part of the service.[11] Death was making substantial inroads in the Purdue family.

On the Purdue campus enrollment had reached a peak of 9,002 resident students; thousands were enrolled in the Army Specialized Training Program, the Navy V-12 and V-5 programs, as well as in the Women's Army Corps Officers Training Program, the School For Apprentice Electricians Mates, and others. Professor H. B. Knoll's account of Purdue's contributions to the war effort presents the record of the university's response to the tremendous demands of the war years.[12] The university was geared to the rapid pace of the war-time situation, and the president's responsibilities had increased accordingly.

Elliott found little time to make either written or oral reports to the alumni, to the students, or to the citizens of the state. Restrictions on travel kept him from meeting with various groups over the state as had been his practice and students who were generally assigned to the Purdue campus for only short time periods were not easy for Elliott to reach in the same way that he had worked with pre-war student groups.

Recognizing that the university had undergone a series of traumatic changes, largely as a result of deaths and the war, Elliott made every effort to bring about a renewed unity of purpose among staff and students alike. But it was virtually an impossible task for many reasons, of course, to restore the old "Spirit of Purdue." There was the rapid turnover in both students and staff, many remaining on campus for no more than a semester; of those who were in classes, many had simply been assigned to Purdue and felt none of the loyalties that were developed in the prewar groups; and the day by day uncertainties of war provided no stability, no strong sense of purpose for either group.

Administrative changes occurred at an unprecedented rate. Dean Jordan had died in April 1941, and had been replaced by a new dean of the School of Pharmacy, Glenn L. Jenkins, in September of that year. Both Dean Dukes of the Graduate School and Dean of Men M. L. Fisher had retired in June 1942, and had been succeeded by Deans E. C. Young and F. I. Goldsmith.

The situation called for strong, vigorous leadership, yet Purdue had been under the guidance of an administrative committee; perhaps any one person from the administrative group could have performed the role; but the committee and even the board, acting under the temporary leadership of vice-president Noel, were caught in a chain of circumstances.

When the fall term opened in 1943 a student-faculty convocation was called by Elliott which was publicized as a "gripe session." The president minced no words as he told the group that he had been delegated authority by the board (on June 8, 1940) to take all steps to see that the university did its utmost to contribute to the war effort. He said bluntly, "The University as a national institution is committed to omit no effort which would contribute to the furthering of our country's goal, which is victory. . . . I challenge you to take it."

With his firm, no-nonsense approach to matters, it seemed that the university community was perhaps more willing to accept the unsettled, even hectic, way of life and continue to do what had to be done with a greater degree of acceptance, even though there was never a return during Elliott's years to the "old Purdue" that he had led so effectively.

As he sought to recapture some of the enthusiasm for the institution that had been so evident among the Purdue grads, Elliott asked the Alumni Association to cooperate with his office in a major effort to reach the alums. A letter of Christmas greetings was sent to graduates who were located in all parts of the world in 1943. The greeting was tremendously well received by most former students and letters of acknowledgment poured in to the Alumni Office. Elliott had touched a responsive chord and succeeded in stirring up memories of Purdue that had been dormant during the long war years.

Partly as a result of this unexpected and warm response, the Purdue Alumni Scholarship Foundation was established September 1, 1944. Although he had not looked with enthusiasm on the proposal when it was first presented by Corydon H. Hall, an active Purdue alumnus residing in Chicago, it finally seemed that the establishment of the fund was an effective way to channel alumni support to provide assistance to athletes and superior students, and Hall was given the job of developing still another allied corporation.

His personal desire to provide financial aid for students had been documented many times; and there had been an Elliott-established student loan fund, called "The President's Fund," at Purdue since November 1923. At the present time it contains slightly more than $1,000 and is only one of many similar funds; but in 1923, when Elliott established the account with an initial gift of $100, it was one of only a few such funds.

The war years almost completely disrupted Elliott's pattern of communicating with students, staff, and others interested in the university. Even the annual reports, which had carried Elliott's meticulous account of the year's activities, beginning with the year 1942-1943 no longer carried the accustomed "President's Review of the Year." Instead, a new publication was adopted which was more colorful, and was designed to attract a larger group of readers. Elliott contributed an essay on the allied corporations and a brief history of the university to the 1942-1943 report. The following year the annual report carried only his brief statement on enrollment figures, the war toll, and a sketchy outline of plans for the future development of the university.

RETIREMENT FROM PURDUE

At a regularly scheduled board meeting on April 20, 1944, Elliott was advised that he should plan to terminate his presidency on June 30, 1945, for in December 1944 he would reach the age of seventy, which was the mandatory retirement age. A two-man committee of the board had been named earlier to begin the search for the seventh president. Although Elliott would probably have been willing to stay on as president until his successor could be found, the final decision was made clear when Hillenbrand announced the date of Elliott's retirement at a special faculty meeting held on December 29, 1944.

During the next six months, many special events were scheduled to honor the retiring president and the newspapers of the state carried articles which praised him highly and recognized the tremendous development of Purdue under his leadership.

The largest single event was a Chamber of Commerce banquet held in the Purdue Memorial Union Building on March 14, 1945. More than 800 guests from all over the nation were assembled to pay tribute to Elliott and Mrs. Elliott, who were accompanied at the banquet by Mrs. Nowland, Mrs. Elliott's 93 year old mother. The speakers included board member William A. Hanley; Chamber of Commerce representative Harry Schultz; student representative Richard Blackhall; alumni representative Burr S. Swezey; and Professor Louis M. Sears, representing the faculty. Preston Calvert and E. B. "Eth" Baugh, executive secretary of the Alumni Association, presided at the gala affair. Many references were made, of course, to Elliott's "dynamic, driving power," and his quick wit.

To many who attended the banquet, the highlight occurred when Professor Sears was finally called on to speak for the faculty. Sears noted that the earlier tributes, "lavish" though they had been, were nonetheless inadequate; but he reminded Elliott, comparing him with Columbus, that "there must have been some sailors on that ship." There was much laughter from the audience but when Elliott's turn came, he pointed out that as "on the voyages of Columbus, his crewmen sometimes mutined, and had been put in irons." While the crowd burst into laughter and applause, Sears slowly shook his head from side to side with a wry smile on his face. It was typical of Elliott to have the last word.

The university had grown in every respect during the twenty-three year period of Elliott's presidency. It is obvious, of course, that it would be impossible to determine how much of the change, if any, could be attributed solely and exclusively to Elliott's leadership. There is considerable evidence that many of the developments were related directly and specifically to the president, while other changes came as a result of actions of students, faculty, the board of trustees, and the legislature working in cooperation with the president; and certainly there were those changes that occurred in spite of the president's actions. Nevertheless, the facts are impressive and those who talked and wrote about Purdue found the occasion of Elliott's retirement a time for comparison.

None of the comparisons that have appeared claim to be completely accurate but, generally speaking, during Elliott's term of office the student enrollment increased from approximately 3,200 to 8,600 students and 20,538 undergraduate and 2,254 advanced degrees were awarded; the number of people employed on the administrative, instructional, and research staffs increased from 456 to 1,247; the number of courses available to students went from 595 to 1,217; the number of major buildings increased from 31 to 59 in 1945; the land acreage available to Purdue increased from 2,784 acres in 1922 to 6,472 acres; and finally, the figure most often quoted, the physical plant value rose from $3,700,000 to $18,-700,000 at the time of Elliott's retirement. Without question, in 1945, under Elliott's leadership, Purdue had been through its greatest period of growth in size, in prestige, and in service.

During his presidency the first comptroller had been employed, a new accounting system had been established, a continuing inventory of university property had been started, and the institution had, for the first time, begun to operate on a strict budget basis. During his early years at Purdue a campus plan had been developed; and all of the existing rules and regulations regarding the internal administration of the university had been codified with the publishing of a university code.

The founding of the allied corporations at Purdue was, without question, one of Elliott's major contributions to higher education in America. The pattern for these corporations, which are legal agencies providing financial support to the university, was first established at Purdue and has been widely imitated in higher educational institutions over the country. The Purdue Research Foundation has become the most productive and the most widely known and can be considered "the prototype for the 30 or 40 which exist today." The significance of these foundations is becoming increasingly apparent to those who follow the affairs of colleges and universities.

The present system of residence halls owned and operated by the university had received its major impetus in 1927 when the legislature authorized the board of trustees to issue bonds for the purpose of erecting income producing properties in the form of student dormitories and residence halls. Equally as important was the long, but eventually successful, court battle between the university and local land-owner Phillip A. (Dick) Russell. The test case had begun in 1926 when condemnation proceedings were initiated to determine whether or not the university had the power of eminent domain. Court rulings were appealed and affirmed, injunctions were filed, appraisals were made and appealed, a change of venue was granted, and the second and third condemnation suits were instituted. Legal proceedings were continued for more than ten years before the Purdue Research Foundation finally was able to contract for the purchase of the land in question. It was not until 1940 that the title was transferred to the university, but the legal questions had been settled, once and for all.

During the twenty-three year period of Elliott's term, many new units had been established to carry on the work of the university: the School of Pharmacy in 1924, the Division of Educational Reference in 1925, the School of Home Economics in 1926, the office of the University Editor in 1927, the Graduate School in 1929, the nation's first university-owned and operated airport in 1930, the Public Safety Institute in 1936, the Joint Highway Research Project in 1937, and the Division of Technical Extension in 1942.

During his administration a retirement plan for faculty members had been established, a plan for sabbatical leaves developed, together with the beginnings of a number of fringe benefits for staff members which included group life insurance, hospitalization insurance, and fee reductions for dependent children.

He had become the great and shining symbol of Purdue to thousands of students and alums who will always have warm and pleasant memories of the university when Elliott was on the scene.

"How anyone could have done more than Elliott did to keep Purdue abreast of the times would be difficult to imagine," wrote Knoll in his notable account of the growth of engineering at Purdue, *The Story of Purdue Engineering,* published nearly 20 years after Elliott's retirement.[13]

> Under Elliott old Purdue became a new Purdue, larger, stronger, and more diverse. In spirit it became restless and dynamic, never quite satisfied with the progress it had made. Elliott drove it onward, dominating the scene and always trying to fulfill the ambitious terms of his personal charter for education. Given what he started with and the opportunities he found, the conclusion is inevitable that he compiled a record of extraordinary achievement. Much of what Purdue became owed its existence to his free, adventurous, and unquenchable spirit.

Final action relative to Elliott's retirement from Purdue came on May 10, 1945, when the board took unprecedented action by creating the office of "President Emeritus of Purdue University" then naming Elliott as president emeritus "for and during his natural life." He was provided with an office in the Executive Building, with secretarial help, and board president John A. Hillenbrand advised Elliott that the Purdue Research Foundation would provide an allowance of $7500 per year (one-half of his annual salary) to be continued during his lifetime without regard for any other retirement income which he might receive.

The matter of selecting a new president was as yet undecided (although they had a promising candidate in mind) and there were at least three persons on the Purdue campus who were eligible for consideration. It was the decision of the board to suspend the rules and create two more new positions, and having done that, they promoted Frank Hockema to vice president and executive dean and R. B. Stewart to vice president and comptroller. Then, by naming Dean Potter acting president, the board made it clear that they were going to bring in as the next president of Purdue a man who had not previously been connected with the university in any way. Elliott was in complete agreement with these actions and was of considerable assistance to the board as they closed out their search for his successor. In August 1945 it was announced that Frederick Lawson Hovde, gifted young scientist-engineer-administrator, had been named as the seventh president of Purdue. He was to assume the office early in January 1946.

The Elliotts, who had been invited to stay in the President's home until it was needed, were asked to surrender the house by November 1, 1946, if possible, in order that it could be renovated before the arrival of the new president. Because Elliott had accepted an assignment to direct a national survey of the pharmacy profession, they decided to move directly to Washington, D.C. from the president's home. They had reached an understanding, however, that when retirement finally came, they would return to Indiana—Lafayette was home. They carefully supervised the inventory of university-owned items in the president's home, and selected and stored virtually all furnishings and personal items and effects before Elliott personally turned over the keys to the university. But even before they were settled in their new apartment at 4701 Connecticut Avenue, N. W., fire swept the warehouse, destroying most of the stored items.

Elliott appeared to accept all of this philosophically, however; it was merely another example of the fate that governed the affairs of men. His retirement, "a passport to oblivion," was merely "the application of the University rule," and the fire "saved somebody a lot of troublesome sorting of the accumulation of the years." He had a new assignment, which is outlined in a later chapter, and with characteristic energy he welcomed the new opportunity for work.

During the next ten years as president emeritus, Elliott was active as a speaker, survey leader, author, and educational consultant; but before any attempt is made to review briefly the activities of his retirement years, consideration must be given to several other areas which held Elliott's interest during his years as president of Purdue University. Though not directly connected with his work at the university, these activities focused attention on Elliott as one of the nation's leaders in higher education.

OTHER INTERESTS

From almost the very beginning of his career in education, Elliott had been intensely interested in boards of control. At Wisconsin, he had worked with local school boards, suggesting ways of improving these agencies and attempting to point out responsibilities of board members. In later years, it was logical that he become concerned with boards of control in higher institutions. His work in this area represents a major attempt to investigate the work of those who govern the higher educational institutions in America. His publications, which are described in the following pages, have become standard references in the field of higher education.

When he went to Montana, Elliott developed a keen interest in the "principal legal agency" created for the purpose of controlling higher schools. Then in 1927 he was asked by R. A. Kent to prepare a chapter on boards of control for a proposed book to be entitled *Higher Education in America*. With Kent as editor, the book was published in 1930. Twenty-two topics were presented by various authors in an attempt to deal with the objective features of curricula and organization and administration of higher education.

The first section of Elliott's chapter was devoted to a thorough review of the historical development of boards of control in America. After describing the governmental device as it existed generally, he then analyzed and listed the various types of boards and their duties, and proceeded to outline certain standards regarding size of the board, constituency, terms of service, organization, and responsibilities. Elliott thought that a board having from seven to fifteen members, serving relatively long terms (10 years), and subject to gradual replacement had the best chance of becoming an effective organization.

Concerning the membership, he noted that only forceful and forward-looking persons who had been successful in their own fields should become members of the board. And in addition, these persons should have the time to enable them to study and understand the activities and aspirations of the institution which they were to serve.

Although it was the general practice for boards to carry on their work through standing committees, Elliott was not in full agreement with the commonly-established policy. When the work of the board was divided and assigned to special committees, he wrote, the board ceased to function as a whole and only a small section of the membership was involved in certain problems. Some ten years later after working at Purdue with a board which had only one committee, a finance and executive committee, he was of the opinion that the board should sit as a committee of the whole upon all matters. A second weakness of the committee system was that industrious and ambitious committees often failed to observe the "all-important difference between those things which belonged to government and those which fall in the province of administration."

Elliott observed that boards met too infrequently, generally speaking, so that too large a proportion of their time and energy was given to routine matters, and too little time was given to considering the results of the work of the institution. He concluded his general comments with a list of "inescapable obligations" of a competent board of control and thus formulated for himself, as well as others, what he felt to be the proper relationship among boards of control, principal executive officers of the institution, and faculties and students.

A number of writers had been critical during the previous decade of the make-up of boards of control. Scott Nearing in 1917 had charged that "college and university boards are almost completely dominated by merchants, manufacturers, capitalists, corporation officials, bankers, doctors, lawyers, educators, and ministers." The following year Veblen's *The Higher Learning in America*[14] cited examples of businessman supremacy on boards; and in 1923 Upton Sinclair's *The Goose Step* compared lists of directors of large corporations with lists of college and university trustees. In 1927, the same year that Elliott wrote his essay for Kent, Earl J. McGrath's study led him to conclude that "the control of higher education in America, both public and private, has been placed in the hands of a small group of the population, namely financiers and business men."

In the face of these kinds of charges Elliott suggested to the Carnegie Foundation, also in 1927, that still another study should be made of boards of control which might blunt the attacks to a degree. While the suggestion was generally approved at that time, the plan was not carried out for several years.

Meanwhile, Henry Suzzalo became president of the Carnegie Foundation for the Advancement of Teaching in 1930, and he and Elliott developed a plan for publishing a work on the legal grounding of higher education, an undertaking indirectly related to boards of control. M. M. Chambers, then a fellow at Ohio State University, was selected to work with Elliott on the project which was not unlike the work Elliott had done in 1906 relating to public school laws. Funds were provided under a series of Carnegie Foundation grants to Purdue University. The product of this initial work for the foundation was *Charters and Basic Laws of Selected American Universities and Colleges,* published in 1934.

The volume contained a collection of charters and certain basic laws of 51 representative American universities, colleges, and technical schools. In addition to constitutional provisions and laws, brief annotations were made of certain significant court decisions. One reviewer wrote that the work served to give the careful reader a comprehensive understanding of the legal basis of higher education in this country—an understanding much needed, it was felt, by the practical administrator as well as the student of the theory of higher education.

The following year (1935) *The Government of Higher Education* by Elliott, Chambers, and W. A. Ashbrook, was published. While this volume was published commercially, Elliott acknowledged the part played by the Carnegie Foundation in financing the original study and credited Suzzalo, Walter Jessup, and Howard J. Savage (all of the Carnegie Foundation) for much assistance. The book was designed by the authors for the special use of trustees in American universities and colleges.

In his preface Elliott wrote that the book was "the outcome of personal convictions developed through a number of years of varied experience, in different parts of the country, with the membership and activities of governing boards of American institutions of higher education." In his opinion the professional educators had given far too little attention to this matter of control of higher education as it is exercised by lay boards of control.

Recognizing that the AAUP and various individuals at that time were contending that lay boards and trustees should delegate much of their authority to faculty members, Elliott concluded that lay boards were going to continue to exercise control, and therefore, those involved in higher education must learn to live and work with the legally constituted groups of laymen.

The Government of Higher Education was prepared as a handbook to be used primarily by board members and was dedicated by Elliott to "the members of the governing boards of American colleges and universities who unselfishly serve as THE SENTINELS OF COMMON SENSE TO GUARD THE GATES OF THE PLACES OF UNCOMMON SENSE." It consisted of 554 questions and answers arranged in twenty-three chapters, almost all of which were concerned with the composition, organization, and functioning of such boards.

The reviews were generally quite favorable. David Spence Hill wrote that the handbook would likely remain the standard manual of reference and guide to laymen interested in higher education. He also suggested that it would be helpful if another manual for trustees, similar to *The Government of Higher Education,* but relating to the boards which control only elementary and secondary education, could be prepared by Elliott, who, he noted, had "run the whole gamut of educational administration in this country."

The Colleges and The Courts, published the following year (1936) by the Carnegie Foundation, was the first volume in a series of studies to assemble and classify legal decisions pertaining to higher education. Elliott and Chambers had organized various sections to consider student admission, discipline, suspension, scholarship, diplomas, and degrees; laws affecting the faculty, the president, and other employees; and the separate conditions of state, municipal, and private higher schools, as well as constitutional provisions regarding universities and colleges. Five years later a second compendium in the series was published by the foundation called *The Colleges and The Courts—1936-1940* prepared by Chambers. Elliott's preface to this study lauded Chambers' work and pointed out that this volume dealt with judicial decisions from 1936 to 1940.

Elliott prepared a preface for each of the two ensuing volumes in the series, *The Colleges and The Courts, 1941-1945* and *1946-1950.* Savage later wrote that "college and university administrators and even lawyers have testified to the usefulness and accuracy of these studies" which were developed by the Elliott-Chambers team.

In 1939 the Carnegie Foundation published *Charters of Philanthropy,* a volume prepared by Elliott and Chambers and lithoprinted for private circulation. The purpose of the book was to facilitate study of the legal basis of American foundations. It reproduced trust instruments, corporate charters, and by-laws of twenty-nine foundations, with a brief analytical introduction comparing some of the salient features of those documents. Nine years later the foundation published a second study with the same title, *Charters of Philanthropy,* which Chambers authored. This second volume contained materials similar to the first, without the restricted material which had limited the original circulation.

In addition to his work with the Carnegie Foundation on these publications, Elliott also served effectively as a trustee of the foundation from 1934 to 1945, and as chairman of the board of trustees from 1943-1945. Although Elliott wrote very little about his own work with the board of the foundation, an account of his valuable contributions is included in Savages' story of the Carnegie Foundation, *The Fruit of An Impulse.*[15]

In 1947, two years after he had retired from the presidency of Purdue, Elliott had an opportunity to review his earlier study of boards of control, and to present his mature conclusions with regard to an effective board of control. The occasion for this review was his address before the Institute for Administrative Officers of Higher Institutions. Although it had been twenty years since his first study of the government of American higher education institutions had been made, he felt that the passing of the years and the many changes in the extent and goals of higher education had "furnished no basis for any essential changes of the first judgment."

Noting that there had been some studies which advocated a system for selecting board members so that the membership would represent various interest groups, Elliott concluded that there was no system which had his complete confidence; that there was no wholly dependable procedure. Whatever the method, whether appointment by governors, or election by the people in the case of publicly controlled institutions, or through co-optation, there is no guarantee that the superior individual will be named, he felt.

Concluding his address, he outlined his feelings that effective boards of control were largely the result of the efforts and skills of the internal leadership of the institution. The president and the faculty, he believed, had the duty of educating the board members with regard to the daily life of the institution.

He had observed many boards of control in action, and it was his conviction that the working effectiveness of a board was largely determined by the working effectiveness of the president of the institution. The president was the activating center of the institution and had the task of training and educating his board. "This may not be difficult," he concluded, but it is "always a delicate undertaking."

Elliott had worked closely with governing boards of higher institutions for nearly thirty years and was well acquainted with the many ramifications of such a "delicate undertaking."

After his initial experiences in Montana with board members, faculty members, and citizens of the state, he reportedly told the governor of that state that a university executive needed "a good, thick skin; a first-class copper-lined stomach; a clear conscience and god-given common sense." But, he concluded, "if you haven't the first two qualities, the last two are as nothing."

As the years went by, Elliott was prompted on a number of occasions to set down his list of presidential qualifications. He was particularly pleased on two occasions at the reception given to his remarks concerning the presidency. His address at the inaugural dinner for President L. B. Hopkins of Wabash College in 1926, for example, was received so well that W. N. Brigance included it in his book, *Classified Speech Models*.[16] Brigance, who attended the ceremony, wrote that the speech held "value as a model to be preserved for study." Elliott was immensely flattered and quite proud that his remarks appeared "between speeches by Mark Twain and Frederick Landis," the latter a U. S. Congressman from Indiana (1903-07) and well known author and columnist.

Then in 1940 at the inaugural dinner for President H. R. Bevis of Ohio State University, Elliott presented his "Decalogue For Presidents" which he hoped would "smooth the long path of service ahead, and give courage for the right; and courage for the wrong when wrong better serves the rights of youth."
His ten pronouncements were as follows:

1. Thou shalt not worship thyself nor thy salary. Neither shalt thou permit thy arteries to be hardened by ambition for higher places.

2. Thou shalt not plume thy plumage in the presence of thy trustees.

3. Thou shalt not covet the scholarship of scholars. Be thou ever mindful that thou art the messenger for and not the master of scholars.

4. Thou shalt multiply and magnify thy powers of limitless patience, resist temptation to speak in public places, and reserve for the silence of thine own study the exercise of thy human right to profane utterance.

5. Thou shalt resolve always to be the welcome companion of students, thereby renewing thine own youth and acquiring the wisdom of life yet to be.

6. Thou shalt not make war on the Fourth Estate. Ever keep in mind the many of your profession who have been torpedoed by printers' type.

7. Thou shalt learn a lesson from the lowly rhinoceros and cultivate a thick impervious epidermis, thereby suffering painlessly the pin pricks and pitchforks of thine enemies and thy critics.

8. Thou shalt not bow down nor worship the idols of pigskins, nor make unto thyself graven images shapened as scoreboards.

9. Thou shalt walk each day not less than five miles alone and out of doors for communion with thy better self.

10. Thou shalt honor thy digestion and preserve the power of thy pancreatic and gastric juices that thy days in office may be long, and filled with the inspirations of well-being. This is the last and the greatest of commandments for wisdom and happiness.

But at the same time Elliott was having fun at the expense of the office of president, he invariably included a serious charge for those who would work with a university president. Practically every address that he made at an inaugural ceremony, from his address at the University of Washington for President Suzzalo in 1916 to his 1955 commencement address (in which he honored Chancellor C. M. Hardin) at the University of Nebraska, included the plea "give this leader full opportunity for exercise of his leadership. Match his courage with your competence, his skill with your sympathy, his power with your patience. Protect him from personal, partisan, political self-seekers that this University may continue to possess an inspired leadership both for men in high and, above all, for men in humble places."

Elliott said on many occasions, "Effective and inspired leadership demands courage, skill, power, and an inexhaustible supply of sheer physical stamina." As one reviews his career in higher education, it becomes readily apparent that Elliott possessed those characteristics. His range of interests and activities were prodigious.

While at Purdue, for example, he served as a member of the Board of Visitors for the U. S. Naval Academy in 1935 and 1936; he was a conciliator in disputes between the United Mine Workers and the Indiana Coal Operators in 1929-1930; he taught during the summer session at Peabody College for Teachers (1930), at Teacher College (1925) and the University of Chicago (1926) having taught at the latter institutions earlier (1907 and 1911, respectively); he was a member of the National Advisory Commission on Education in 1929-1931; he was on the Indiana State Board of Education from 1922 to 1931; and he was a member of the Science Committee of the National Resources Planning Board from 1935 to 1943.

A special project that was particularly satisfying to Elliott was his work in assembling and editing the annual reports of President Nicholas Murray Butler of Columbia University. The volume (published in 1937) was more than a mere tribute to Butler, for Elliott had a firm conviction that the selections from the annual reports would prove serviceable to those "who are yet to wrestle with the intricate issues of higher education." Preparation of the book was no small "extra undertaking."

In addition to the several areas already mentioned and the numerous positions which he held, he also devoted considerable time and effort to still another major activity, surveys in higher education. Elliott had had a significant role in the development of the school survey movement which had its beginning in 1911-1912. Considering his part in the early surveys of secondary schools and state school systems, it is not surprising that Elliott later, when he became an administrator in higher education, was also involved in surveys of higher institutions. The first survey of higher education in which Elliott participated was concerned with the problem of financing the state colleges and universities of the nation. It began at almost the same time that he began his administrative duties at Purdue.

THE EDUCATIONAL FINANCE INQUIRY

Early in 1921 at an N.E.A. Department of Superintendence meeting in Atlantic City, a resolution was introduced calling for a nation-wide inquiry into the cost of public education. As a result of the discussion following this resolution, a committee which included Elliott was named to plan an investigation of the problem of financing public education. In August 1921, the committee met in New York and proposed the Educational Finance Inquiry, a commission to study expenditures at various educational institutions in selected communities. Recognizing the possible value of such a study, the American Council on Education sought contributions for this purpose and raised $170,000.

The members of the commission were George D. Strayer of Columbia University, chairman; Ellwood P. Cubberley, Stanford University; Samuel P. Capen, University of Buffalo and a director of the American Council on Education; Elliott, and others. The original purpose of the inquiry was to study the existing programs of public education, the extent to which these were being carried out, and the costs involved. Although the original plan was to have included a study of the financing of higher education, it was impossible for the investigators to get the cooperation of any sizeable group of state higher institutions, thus the major attention of the inquiry was given to the cost of public elementary and secondary schools.

Elliott reported in 1924 that "when it became evident that the state institutions were long on the theory of facts and very short on the delivery of same," it was necessary to turn to those areas where information could be secured.

In most cases there was not a refusal to give the information, but the inquiry was led to conclude that most institutions simply did not have the financial facts. At Purdue University, for example, as has been noted previously, there was no business office until 1922 when the trustees authorized Elliott to employ the university's first comptroller of finance to act in the capacity of business manager. In a few instances, Elliott noted, certain higher educational institutions had set up accounting and statistical procedures but even those institutions were very reluctant to make available the details of their financial structure to members of the inquiry staff.

While this situation at first promised to prevent the inquiry from making any fact-finding, constructive studies in the field of higher education, a second project was soon outlined which was to make a contribution to the more effective financial administration of tax-supported higher schools. The project was that of developing a simple, common method for the calculation of annual per-student cost of instruction in higher institutions. On May 23, 1922, the Educational Finance Inquiry Commission finally recommended that an intensive study be made of the detailed institutional costs of the higher schools within a certain geographical area. The original proposal called for such study to be made of the state universities, colleges, and normal schools in Montana, Idaho, Oregon, and Washington. But when Elliott moved from Montana to Indiana, the state institutions of Montana and Idaho were dropped from the study while Purdue University was added to the list.

The completed study was published in 1925 as Volume XIII of a series of publications of the Educational Finance Inquiry, and was titled *Unit Costs of Higher Education,* by E. B. Stevens and Elliott. Stevens was the executive secretary of the University of Washington under Suzzalo and had carried on significant pioneer studies of the finances of the higher schools of that state. He was largely responsible for the technical aspects of the report, while Elliott prepared the introductory chapters and acted in an advisory capacity for the total report.

The report contained a detailed description of a technique for the classification of institutional expenditures and the correlation of these expenditures with students and other services. While the Unit Cost Technique never achieved unanimous support, it continues to receive a qualified recognition. The study made by Elliott and Stevens marks one of the earliest attempts to solve an ever-present financial problem of higher education.

Seven years after the study of unit costs was published for the Educational Finance Inquiry, Elliott became associated with another survey group—this time to study higher education in Georgia. The board of regents there invited L. D. Coffman, president of the University of Minnesota, Elliott, Charles H. Judd, dean of the School of Education at the University of Chicago, George F. Zook, then president of the University of Akron and later president of the American Council on Education, and George A. Works, professor of higher education at the University of Chicago, to carry out an investigation of the university system of that state.

The report, which was completed in 1932, provided an analysis of the system of higher schools and made certain recommendations. It is difficult to determine what part Elliott played in organizing the work of the survey, in executing the study, and in preparing the final report. He briefly mentioned the survey in an article for *The Purdue Alumnus,* indicating that he had spent less than a week in Georgia. R. B. Stewart, however, spent a considerable amount of time and effort on the survey.

In 1935 a committee of the Board of Regents of the University of the State of New York organized a special survey called the *Regents' Inquiry into the Character and Cost of Public Education in the State of New York.*

Elliott was asked to direct that part of the inquiry having to do with higher education and adult education. David S. Hill of the Carnegie Foundation was employed to carry out the study of higher education while Floyd W. Reeves of the University of Chicago was in charge of the study of adult education in New York. Their task was to determine the extent of the state's obligation for the provision of higher educational opportunities and what type of regulation the state should exercise over public and private institutions.

As a result of the investigations carried out by Hill and Reeves under Elliott's direction, *Higher Education in the State of New York* with Hill and Elliott as the authors was published in 1937. Two years later the Inquiry published Elliott's brief *Summary Memoranda With Reference To Higher Education.* The study of adult education in New York was completed with the publishing of *Adult Education,* by Reeves, Fansler, and Houle in 1938 which included a preface written by Elliott.

While the details connected with the publication of the above reports were still being discussed, however, another opportunity to conduct a university survey was extended to Elliott. This time the University of the Philippines had resolved to seek help in making a thorough study of all its courses, personnel, and equipment in all colleges and departments. This was the survey, referred to earlier, which took Elliott away from Purdue University for five months. Although he and Packer received many accolades from those with whom they had worked in the Philippines, Elliott was never convinced that the work which he and Packer had done would have any lasting effect.

The next several years saw a decline in the number of university surveys, perhaps largely because unsettled conditions in international affairs made long-range planning more or less impractical. Elliott, for example, had been scheduled to return to the Philippines in 1940 but the impending world crisis stopped that.

Immediately following the war, however, certain states authorized investigations of their state systems of public education. Elliott, of course, at the close of the war had just stepped down as president of Purdue University and with his background in the school survey movement, he was one of the first consultants to fill the demand for capable, experienced educators to help carry out the post-war surveys.

In June 1945, a committee of the State Legislature of West Virginia executed a contract with George D. Strayer of Teachers College to employ a staff to conduct a survey of certain phases of public education in that state. Elliott was selected by Strayer to work in the area of higher education. He was responsible in part for the field work and preparation of that section of the report concerned with West Virginia University. His report was prepared during the month that he was closing out his responsibilities at Purdue University and was finally submitted to the director in September 1945. The final report prepared by Strayer and published by the state late in 1945 contained a section called "Higher Education in West Virginia—the University" which was largely written by Elliott.

Then early the following year, George S. Zook of the American Council on Education asked Elliott to direct a nationwide survey on the pharmacy profession. It was this invitation that led to the Elliott's leaving Lafayette, Indiana, to move to Washington, D.C., where they stayed for more than two years, until July 1948.

NOTES

1. William M. Hepburn and Louis M. Sears, *Purdue University, Fifty Years of Progress* (Indianapolis: The Hollenbeck Press, 1925), p. 131.

2. R. W. Babcock, ed., *Addresses and Records, Semi-Centennial Ceremonial, Purdue University, May 1924* (Indianapolis: Wm. B. Burford Printing Company, 1928).

3. Floyd W. Reeves et al., *Report of a Survey of the State Institutions of Higher Learning in Indiana* (Indianapolis: Wm. B. Burford Printing Company, 1926).

4. Fred C. Kelly, *David Ross, modern pioneer* (New York: A. A. Knopf, 1946).

5. G. Stanley Meikle, "The Genesis and Organization of Research as a Function of Education of Purdue University. Historical Summaries," *Report of the President and Research Director, Purdue Research Foundation,* May 12, 1954 (unpublished paper prepared at Purdue University, May 12, 1954).

6. Babcock, *Purdue University, 1922-32* (Lafayette: published by the university, 1933).

7. George Palmer Putnam, *Soaring Wings* (New York: Harcourt Brace and Company, 1939), p. 272.

8. ——, *Wide Margins* (New York: Harcourt Brace and Company, 1942), p. 175.

9. Helen Hand and Thomas R. Johnson, ed., *The Trustees and the Officers of Purdue University,* 1865-1940 (Lafayette: published by the university, 1940), pp. 425-26.

10. Henry C. Herge and others, *Wartime College Training Programs of the Armed Services* (Washington: American Council on Education, 1948).

11. Fred C. Kelly, *George Ade, warmhearted satirist* (Indianapolis: The Bobbs-Merrill Company, 1947), p. 265.

12. H. B. Knoll, ed., *1941-1945, A Record of a University in the War Years, The Archives of Purdue, No. 4* (Lafayette: published by the university, 1947).

13. ——, *The Story of Purdue Engineering* (Lafayette: Purdue University Studies, 1963).

14. Thorstein Veblen, *The Higher Learning in America* (New York: A. M. Kelley, 1965).

15. Howard J. Savage, *Fruit of an Impulse* (New York: Harcourt Brace and Company, 1953).

16. W. Norwood Brigance, ed., *Classified Speech Models* (New York: F. S. Crofts and Company, 1928), p. 306.

CHAPTER 5

The Later Years

"My fifth career was spent as a servant of the profession of Pharmacy," Elliott said as he reviewed his career, obviously pleased that he had been selected to direct a nation-wide survey even though he was 70 years old, presumably scheduled for a quiet retirement.

His first professional activity, he recalled, had been as a chemist. Second, as a public school teacher, he found himself a "chemical apostate," and later moved on to a third, a decade of teaching in the university.

For a fourth career, he had been "lured into that chaos of high-grade clerical activity commonly called executive work" where he spent nearly thirty years as a university head, "surviving only through the advantage of the blood stream of stout forebears." But survive and prosper he did, and when he embarked on his "fifth career," he was as eager to work as he had been when he began his first.

THE PHARMACEUTICAL SURVEY

The Pharmaceutical Survey was originally planned by the American Association of Colleges of Pharmacy. That organization wanted a complete survey made of pharmaceutical education as well as pharmaceutical practice. The association, after deciding that the American Council on Education was the best qualified agency to do the job, secured funds to underwrite the cost of the study from a third group, the American Foundation for Pharmaceutical Education.

Elliott was selected by the council to direct the survey, and a general statement was prepared jointly by the three sponsoring agencies which announced that, "Because of the important role that pharmacy plays in American life, because pharmaceutical services are constantly being expanded, and because pharmaceutical education has expanded until there are at present [1946] approximately 65 schools of pharmacy in the country, it is important that a study be made of pharmacy and pharmaceutical services. . ."

Elliott's association with the American Council on Education had begun in 1921 with the Educational Finance Inquiry. He had long been active in promoting the affairs of the council, having served as chairman in 1937-38, so it was not surprising for the group to turn to Elliott when the survey of the pharmacy profession was proposed.

According to Elliott, who summarized the mandate which was issued to the director, the survey was (1) to determine what pharmacists do in practice; (2) to determine what the pharmacist should know in order to perform the duties indicated in number (1); (3) to determine what the colleges should teach in order to fit pharmacists for the work they are expected to do; (4) to determine what the pharmacist is expected to do, what he must know, and what the college must teach in reference to the several types of positions in industry, government service, army, navy, etc.; (5) to determine trends which may indicate what pharmacists will do in the future, and (6) to determine the economic status of pharmacists.

It was originally planned that the survey would take approximately two years to complete, but within a few months after the study began, the period was extended to three years (1946-1949). Two years were to be spent in gathering and interpreting the facts, while the third year was to be devoted to putting the recommendations into effect.

The survey staff, with the help of a national committee representative of the entire area of pharmaceutical activities, was able to complete the study on schedule. During the course of the survey Elliott traveled more than 40,000 miles visiting 30 colleges of pharmacy in all parts of the nation. In 1950 *The General Report of the Pharmaceutical Survey, 1946-1949* (written by Elliott) was published by the American Council on Education. Two years later the second and final report, *The Pharmaceutical Curriculum,* was completed by L. E. Blauch and G. L. Webster of the survey staff.

In 1950 the American Foundation for Pharmaceutical Education created the office of Director of Educational Relations as recommended by the survey, and named Elliott acting director. He held the post until he resigned in 1952 at the age of 77.

AN EDUCATIONAL CONSULTANT

In 1953 he accepted his last assignment as an educational consultant to the Commanding General of the Army Ordnance Corps. The part-time position required that he visit Aberdeen Proving Grounds in Maryland with some frequency and occasionally travel to other training centers; he was seldom away from Lafayette for more than a few days on any single trip, however.

He continued with this work for three years but gave it up largely because he was simply tired of traveling. In April 1956, he made his last trip to Maryland to receive the nation's Award of Meritorious Civilian Service for his work with the Ordnance Training Command, Major General J. L. Holman, commanding general of the proving ground, made the presentation of the silver lapel pin and certificate.

Early in 1948, having completed much of the work of directing the pharmaceutical survey, the Elliotts began to think seriously about returning to Lafayette. When Frank Hockema learned that local builder L. A. Thise was converting the handsome O. W. Pierce residence into apartments, he quickly suggested that the Elliotts might be interested. Mrs. Elliott knew the home and a single visit with the owner was all that was needed to settle the matter. In July 1948, they moved to the spacious ground floor apartment at 538 South Seventh Street in Lafayette, just across the street and a few houses south of the president's home.

AT HOME

After the move was completed, Elliott was at home most of the time with Mrs. Elliott, busy with his reading and his correspondence. He generally arose early, enjoyed a hearty breakfast, read the morning paper, then drove to his office in the Executive Building, where he looked over the mail, dictated replies to the many letters from acquaintances (he had been an active member of more than 25 national, state, and municipal educational, scientific, and honorary organizations), and frequently wrote portions of his reports for the Ordnance Corps during this period of the day.

His general pattern was to be in the office from about 10:00 a.m. until noon or a little after, then home for the rest of the day. He seemed to adapt quite easily to the more leisurely pace; he kept busy without any special effort, continuing his frequent walks, sometimes accompanied by Mrs. Elliott but more often alone, occasionally doing the shopping for groceries at the neighborhood store, and reading stacks of papers, magazines, and books, almost as though he was fearful of being uninformed about current affairs.

He always had been an avid reader whose interests covered a wide range of topics. Several years earlier, when Elliott was asked by one of the editors of the *Purdue Alumnus* to prepare a list of books that he would recommend, he came up with ten titles. Dubbing these volumes his "Five Pound Shelf of Books," (with no apologies to Harvard's Charles W. Eliot) Elliott urged Purdue students, past and present, to read *Humanizing of Knowledge,* by J. H. Robinson; *On Vital Reserves,* by William James; *Meditations,* Marcus Aurelius; *On Liberty and Other Essays,* John Stuart Mills; *Paracelsus,* Robert Browning; *Twenty-three Tales,* Tolstoi; as well as Shakespeare's *Hamlet,* Emerson's *Compensation,* and Whitman's *Leaves of Grass.*

Some years later (1940) he added "ten little books" to his original list for a total of 20 volumes that he considered exceptional reading. The additions included: Malthus, *The Principle of Population;* Turner, *The Significance of the Frontier in American History;* Coit, *Is Civilization a Disease;* Eliot, *The Conflict Between Individualism and Collectivism in a Democracy;* Shaw, *Socialism and Superior Brains;* Jordan, *The Blood of the Nation;* Winship, *Jukes-Edwards;* Emerson, *On Education;* Newman, *On University Education;* Cicero, *De Amicitia.*

Elliott advised one of his visitors that he expected to re-read *all* of those "good books" now that he had the time; but he also read paperback "who-dun-it" mysteries just for fun, a practice he had followed for many years, especially when traveling on university business.

For nearly ten years after his Purdue career ended, Elliott and Mrs. Elliott thoroughly enjoyed retirement and each other's company; they had been devoted to each other for more than 40 years and for the first time they were able to be together almost without interruption. They loved to talk—about books, people, ideas—and time was never heavy on their hands.

Elliott loved to play cribbage. He had learned the game from his parents as a youngster and had boasted of one cribbage marathon while in college that lasted one hundred games. Whenever his parents came to visit, in Madison, Helena, or Lafayette, they brought their cribbage board and Elliott played with them as he later played with his children and grandchildren. It was his favorite indoor game; the only one he played with real enthusiasm. Mrs. Elliott was not a cribbage fan, however; her game was bridge. So as a compromise, they took up canasta and it became their favorite game together.

Both enjoyed remarkably good health during those years; but on January 9, 1955, after several months of failing health, Mrs. Elliott died at home. Her husband, then 80 years old, and their four children survived. Elliott and Mrs. Elliott had agreed that neither wanted an elaborate funeral and that the services would be simple and private, limited to members of the immediate family. Her body was taken to a local funeral home, then to Indianapolis where private services were conducted by the Reverend Benjamin W. Tinsley, rector of St. John's Episcopal Church in Lafayette, at Christ's Church Cathedral on Monument Circle. The Reverend Reese F. Thornton, Tinsley's predecessor at St. John's who had served as rector from 1931 to 1951, also participated in the service at the request of the family. Following this the remains were taken to an Indianapolis crematorium where a second service was attended only by members of the immediate family. The ashes were returned to Lafayette. Many months went by before Elliott selected a lot in a local cemetery which suited him, and it was not until April 20, 1957, that Mrs. Elliott's remains were interred with simple ceremony.

Mrs. Elliott had made many, many friends in Lafayette and was greatly admired by everyone who knew her. "She was a refined lady;" one acquaintance remarked in my presence. "A lovely person for whom everyone felt great respect and affection." An active leader in the social life of the university and in her church, she also had worked on many community projects and had been honored for her services with the local Red Cross chapter. Shortly after her death, a memorial volume, a missal (containing the Holy Communion service), was placed in St. John's Episcopal Church, and the Elizabeth Nowland Elliott Scholarship Fund was established at Purdue to accept the contributions sent by staff members and other friends of the Elliotts. This fund, now increased to nearly $3,000, is maintained by the Purdue Alumni Scholarship Foundation. A similar fund, the Edward C. Elliott Scholarship Fund, established in 1949 with a $1,000 gift from Mr. and Mrs. Walter Scholer, Sr., presently contains more than $7,000.

Elliott's way of life was changed, of course, after Mrs. Elliott's death, but he continued to live in the apartment, relying more and more on the help of Mrs. Elsie Goetz, who had faithfully served the Elliotts as cook, housekeeper, and occasionally as a practical nurse for many years. He was determined to keep busy and follow as many of his old interests as he could possibly schedule.

Only a few weeks after Mrs. Elliott's death he received an invitation to return to the University of Nebraska to deliver the spring commencement address. Because the occasion was the 60th anniversary of his own graduation, Elliott was particularly pleased to accept the invitation. It was his last major address, filled with reminiscences and excerpts from many of his earlier speeches, yet significant, perhaps, because he chose to include a reiteration of his "personal charter," first stated nearly forty years earlier, that:

> . . . such an institution as this will not have served its purpose until the vast majority of the people of the state, of whatever class or occupation, come freely and fully to know that this, their University is a dependable agency, ever at their disposal, to meet the scientific and educational needs for their happiness, the satisfactions and ideals of their lives; until there is firmly established among those who labor, those who lead, those who learn, and those who teach, that human work makes education possible, and that education in turn must dignify all human work.
>
> "Then and there I stood," he concluded, "Now and there I stand."

Upon his return from the Nebraska trip Elliott contacted his brothers, Fred and Ben, suggesting that the three of them set up an award at the North Platte High School as a memorial to their parents. There was complete agreement, so in 1956 they gave $5,000 to the North Platte School Board to be held in trust; the income was to be used to provide an annual cash award, known as "The Fred and Susan Elliott Pioneer Memorial Award," to an outstanding senior boy or girl "in recognition of the qualities of character, self-reliance, courage, independence, leadership." Arrangements were completed early in 1956 and the award has been made annually since the first certificate was presented in May of that year.

Elliott continued to enjoy good health and was in excellent physical condition for a man of his age until he approached his 83rd year. In October 1957, however, while attending the 55th wedding anniversary of his brother Fred and his wife in Omaha, Nebraska, he suffered a moderate stroke. He was flown back to

Lafayette in a Purdue Aeronautics Corporation plane accompanied by members of the family and Dr. L. W. Combs, director of the Purdue Student Health Center and former athlete at the university.

Elliott made a partial recovery from the effects of the stroke but was an invalid for the remaining three years of his life. Partially paralyzed on his right side, he spent most of his waking hours in a wheel chair, his mind and his spirits seemingly undaunted.

Despite his disability, he was well enough to visit with all of his four children and their families when they gathered in Lafayette for his 83rd birthday on December 21, 1957. Many of his close friends dropped in for a brief greeting during the day.

A month later the Purdue Board of Trustees suspended their rules which prohibited naming a building for any person until 10 years after his death and voted unanimously to re-name the Hall of Music the Edward C. Elliott Hall of Music. It was a high tribute (it is the only Purdue building named for a past president) and the news media publicized the event widely. "The Hall of Music was distinctly an Elliott-conceived idea," said R. B. Stewart in commenting on the board action. "Dr. Elliott envisioned the Hall of Music as not only a great cultural center for Purdue students and staff but also to serve the cultural interests of the community and the state."

When notified of the action at his home, Elliott, who was not unaccustomed to receiving accolades, said simply, "It is the most exceptional honor that has come to me throughout my life." A bronze marker was later placed on the building named to honor "him whose vision and leadership as president of the university brought this structure from a dream into reality to enrich the lives of all who enter."

During the years that he was confined to his home, hundreds of friends came to visit with Elliott and a day seldom passed without several persons dropping in. Even though Elliott never completely adjusted to life as an invalid, he loved having visitors and made a valiant effort to handle his disability as no more than an inconvenience.

Ed Elliott commented that "no university from the president on down ever did more for and tried harder to please its retired president than Purdue did for my dad." Among those staff members who frequently stopped by were President Hovde and his wife, "Eth" Baugh, "Tommy" Johnston, "Red" Mackey, "Al" Stewart with some Glee Club boys, George Davis bringing bouquets of gladiolas when they were in bloom, Dean Potter, and the R. B. Stewarts. "It is not possible to enumerate all the people or the many kind things that were done to brighten his days in one way or another," Ed wrote.

Elliott was reluctant to leave home for any reason, but allowed himself to be persuaded to attend the annual John Purdue Club outing in both 1958 and 1959. Athletic Director Mackey and all the coaches, former athletes, and Purdue sports enthusiasts made every effort to see that he enjoyed himself; even though it was difficult for him to move about, he occasionally saw a football game either from his car, parked high above the end zone, or from his wheel chair. The last game he attended matched Purdue against Nebraska, his alma mater—and Purdue won.

On his 84th birthday, Geneva Nugent, foods manager at the Purdue Memorial Union, brought a cake, which she had baked, to a small party attended by son John and his family together with Mr. and Mrs. R. B. Stewart, who had provided the dinner, Johnston, Baugh, and university photographer Julian "Jake" Jacobson. Other visitors came during the day and the local paper later carried the story and pictures. An editorial entitled "Elder Statesman" noted that "Purdue's grand old man serves as a dynamic link with the past and an inspiration to future achievements."

Recognizing that death was probably not far distant, Elliott was determined that his passing should not inconvenience those who were closest to him. Sometime after Mrs. Elliott's death, he had told his son John that all arrangements relative to his own death had been made with his physician Dr. R. P. Gripe, a local funeral director, cemetery officials, and Mr. Tinsley. There was to be no public funeral.

The decision eliminated the need for others to decide when and where a ceremony should be held, whether or not it should be public or private, what to do about flowers, invitation lists, music, and all of the matters which might be associated with a public ceremony.

Proceeding in his typically meticulous manner, he had detailed the arrangements in writing and referred to these instructions, kept with his will and other papers, as his "end papers." When John suggested that there might be some pressure exerted by the university and friends to hold public services, Elliott advised him he would discuss the matter with President Hovde who would respect Elliott's wishes.

A local attorney, Roger D. Branigin, assisted Elliott in the writing of his will which simply divided the estate among the four children. All the materials kept at Purdue were left to the university, but there were two special bequests: $1,000 was left to Purdue Musical Organizations, and $1,000 was left to St. John's Episcopal Church in Lafayette. The latter amount was to be held in perpetuity to provide that flowers be placed at the altar on the first Sunday in each October. Mrs. Elliott's birthday was October 3, 1875.

Shortly before his death, Elliott prepared a memorandum to his children in which he indicated that certain personal items and furnishings in the home either belonged to or were intended for certain members of the family or for specific friends. He planned exceedingly well and every wish was carried out without problems.

When Elliott died on June 16, 1960, at the age of 85, his body was taken from the hospital, where he had been committed two days earlier, to a local funeral home in accordance with his instructions. Private communion services were held two days later at St. John's Church, attended only by his children and their families together with his two brothers and members of their families. His body was then taken to the Indianapolis crematorium and his ashes were later returned to the funeral home in Lafayette.

On Saturday, July 30, 1960, the children were present at a brief service conducted by Mr. Tinsley in Rest Haven Memorial Park in Lafayette where Elliott's remains were buried beside those of Mrs. Elliott. A simple bronze plate is imbedded in the ground to mark the location.

Only a handful of people have known of the circumstances surrounding Elliott's death, but thousands have known of his life and have benefitted from his lifetime of service to education.

Notwithstanding all that has been said and written about Elliott, President Hovde, who was eminently well qualified to assess Elliott's work during the peak years of his career, may have provided the most appropriate and insightful epitaph when he said simply,

"He made the university live in the hearts and minds of the people of this state. . . ."

A Selected Bibliography of the Works of Edward Charles Elliott

1899 —

> *By-Laws and Rules and Regulations of the Public Schools of the City of Leadville, Colorado.* Leadville, Colorado: Leadville Publishing and Printing Company, 1899.

1900 —

> *Courses of Study for the Leadville High School.* Leadville, Colorado: Leadville Publishing and Printing Company, 1900.

> *Courses of Study for the Leadville Public Schools.* Leadville, Colorado: Leadville Publishing and Printing Company, 1900.

1901 —

> *Annual Report of the Board of Directors for the year ending June 30, 1901.* Leadville, Colorado: Leadville Publishing and Printing Company, 1901.

1902 —

> *Annual Report of the Board of Directors for the year ending June 30, 1902.* Leadville, Colorado: Leadville Publishing and Printing Company, 1902.

1903 —

> *Annual Report of the Board of Directors for the year ending June 30, 1903.* Leadville, Colorado: Leadville Publishing and Printing Company, 1903.

1905 —

> "The Genesis of American Secondary Schools in Their Relation to the Life of the People," *The Fourth Yearbook of the National Society for the Scientific Study of Education, Part I.* Chicago: University of Chicago Press, 1905, pp. 11-26.

> *Some Fiscal Aspects of Public Education in American Cities.* (Teachers College Contributions to Education, No. 6.) New York: Columbia University, 1905.

1906 —

> *State School Systems: Legislation and Judicial Decisions Relating to Public Education, October 1, 1906, to October 1, 1908.* (Bureau of Education, Bulletin No. 3.) Washington, D. C.: United States Government Printing Office, 1906.

1907 —

> "A Type of Positive Educational Reform," *Educational Review,* 33:344 - 355, April, 1907.

> "Education Raised to the Third Power," (Part I), *Wisconsin Journal of Education,* 39:278 - 280, October, 1907.

"Education Raised to the Third Power," (Part II), *Wisconsin Journal of Education,* 39:318 - 321, November, 1907.

"Education Raised to the Third Power," (Part III), *Wisconsin Journal of Education,* 39:358 - 360, December, 1907.

1908 —

Report of the Course for the Training of Teachers for the Biennial Period Ending June 30, 1908. (Bulletin of the University of Wisconsin, No. 273, General Series No. 150.) Madison, Wisconsin: Published by the University, 1908, pp. 75-91.

State School Systems II: Legislation and Judicial Decisions Relating to Public Education, October 1, 1906, to October 1, 1908. (Bureau of Education, Bulletin No. 7.) Washington, D. C.: United States Government Printing Office, 1908.

"The Equality of Opportunity—How Secured," *The Proceedings of the Department of Superintendence, National Education Association.* Washington, D. C.: Government Printing Office, 1908, pp. 46-48.

1909 —

"Some Problems of the Rural School Situation," (Part I), *Atlantic Educational Journal,* 4:13-14, February, 1909.

"Some Problems of the Rural School Situation," (Part II), *Atlantic Educational Journal,* 4:16-17, 21 March, 1909.

"Some Problems of the Rural School Situation," (Part III), *Atlantic Educational Journal,* 4:17-18, 30 May, 1909.

"Some Problems of the Rural School Situation," (Part IV), *Atlantic Educational Journal,* 4:12-13, 22 June, 1909.

"Educational Advancement and the New Federalism," *Educational Review,* 38:217-225, October, 1909.

"Introduction," *The Relative Standings of Pupils in the High School and in the University,* by Walter Feno Dearborn. (Bulletin of the University of Wisconsin, No. 312, High School Series, No. 6.) Madison, Wisconsin: Published by the University, 1909, pp. 5-6.

Industrial Education. (Legislative Summary No. 1.) Madison, Wisconsin: The American Association for Labor Legislation, 1909.

1910 —

Report of the Course for the Training of Teachers for the Biennial Period Ending June 30, 1910. (Bulletin of the University of Wisconsin, No. 411, General Series No. 257.) Madison, Wisconsin: Published by the University, 1910, pp. 95-119.

"The State University and the University State," *The University of Idaho Bulletin,* 5:1-11, November, 1910.

"The Training of Teachers," *The Wisconsin Alumni Magazine,* 12:51-54, November, 1910.

Industrial Education. (Legislative Summary No. 2.) New York: American Association for Labor Legislation, 1910.

"Education, Review of Legislation, 1907-08," *New York State Library, 91st Annual Report, 1908, volume 3, supplement 8.* Albany: University of the State of New York, 1910, pp. 171-190.

State School Systems III: Legislation and Judicial Decisions Relating to Public Education, October 1, 1908, to October 1, 1909. (Bureau of Education, Bulletin No. 2.) Washington, D. C.: United States Government Printing Office, 1910.

Legislation Upon Industrial Education in the United States. (Bulletin No. 12, National Society for the Promotion of Industrial Education.) New York: Published by the society, 1910. (With C. A. Prosser)

"University Courses in Educational Administration," *The Aims, Scope, and Methods of a University Course in Public School Administration.* Iowa City: C. A. Webber Printing Company, 1910, pp. 73-94.

"Report of Chairman of the Committee on Accredited Schools," *Report of the Regents of the University of Wisconsin, 1908-1910.* Madison, Wisconsin: Published by the University, 1910, pp. 253-255.

Outline of a Tentative Scheme for the Measurement of Teaching Efficiency. Madison, Wisconsin: Democrat Printing Co., 1910.

1911 —

"A Model Secondary School," *The Wisconsin Alumni Magazine,* 12:257-259, March, 1911.

"Training the Teacher," *Atlantic Educational Journal,* 7:13, September, 1911.

"School Budget," *A Cyclopedia of Education,* Vol. I. Paul Monroe, editor; New York: The Macmillan Company, 1911, pp. 461-464.

"City School Administration," *A Cyclopedia of Education,* Vol. II. Paul Monroe, editor; New York: The Macmillan Company, 1911, pp. 16-22.

"School Board Conventions," *A Cyclopedia of Education,* Vol. II. Paul Monroe, editor; New York: The Macmillan Company, 1911, p. 201.

"Recent American Educational Commissions," *A Cyclopedia of Education,* Vol. III. Paul Monroe, editor; New York: The Macmillan Company, 1911, pp. 154-156.

"Cooperative Research Within the Field of Education: Its Organization and Encouragement," *The School Review Monographs, No. I.* National Society of College Teachers of Education. Chicago: University of Chicago Press, 1911, pp. 57-59.

1912 —

Report of the Course for the Training of Teachers for the Biennial Period Ending June 30, 1912. (Bulletin of the University of Wisconsin, No. 562, General Series No. 287.) Madison, Wisconsin: Published by the University, 1912.

Report of the Committee on Accredited Schools and Appointments for the Biennial Period Ending June 30, 1912. (Bulletin of the University of Wisconsin, No. 564, General Series No. 389.) Madison, Wisconsin: Published by the University, 1912.

"Reliability of the Grading of High School Work in English," *The School Review,* 20:442-457, September, 1912. (With Daniel Starch)

"The System of General Supervision and the Board of Examiners," *Report of Committee on School Inquiry, Vol. II, 1911-1912,* New York City Board of Estimate and Apportionment. New York: Published by the City, 1912, pp. 315-456.

"The Rural School of Today," *Journal of Proceedings and Addresses of the Fiftieth Annual Meeting of the National Education Association of the United States.* Washington, D. C.: Government Printing Office, 1912, pp. 558-559.

"Standards of Tests of Efficiency," *Journal of Proceedings and Addresses of the Fiftieth Annual Meeting of the National Education Association of the United States.* Washington, D. C.: Government Printing Office, 1912, pp. 564-566.

"State University and Public Instruction," *Journal of Proceedings and Addresses of the Fiftieth Annual Meeting of the National Education Association of the United States.* Washington, D. C.: Government Printing Office, 1912, pp. 781-783.

"Instruction: Its Organization and Control," *High School Education.* C. H Johnston, editor; New York: Scribners, 1912, pp. 106-127.

1913 —

"The Report of the New York School Inquiry," *The Elementary School Teacher,* 13:320-325, March, 1913.

"Reliability of Grading Work in Mathematics," *The School Review,* 21:254-259, April, 1913. (With Daniel Starch)

"The Proposed Supervisory Council for the New York Schools," *The American Teacher,* 2:66-68, May, 1913.

"General Supervision," *The American Teacher,* 2:92-93, June, 1913.

"Reliability of Grading Work in History," *The School Review,* 21:676-681, December, 1913. (With Daniel Starch)

"The School House as a Crime Contributor," *Bulletin of the American Academy of Medicine,* 14:383-387, December, 1913.

"National Government of the United States and Education," *A Cyclopedia of Education,* Vol. IV. Paul Monroe, editor; New York: The Macmillan Company, 1913, pp. 372-382.

"Teachers Pensions," *A Cyclopedia of Education,* Vol. IV. Paul Monroe, editor; New York: The Macmillan Company, 1913, pp. 635-640.

"Appointment of Teachers," *A Cyclopedia of Education,* Vol. V. Paul Monroe, editor; New York: The Macmillan Company, 1913, pp. 500-503.

"Promotion of Teachers," *A Cyclopedia of Education,* Vol. V. Paul Monroe, editor; New York: The Macmillan Company, 1913, pp. 504-506.

"Salaries of Teachers," *A Cyclopedia of Education,* Vol. V. Paul Monroe, editor; New York: The Macmillan Company, 1913, pp. 508-513.

"Sex of Teachers," *A Cyclopedia of Education,* Vol. V. Paul Monroe, editor; New York: The Macmillan Company, 1913, pp. 513-515.

"The Magnified School," *The Social Center.* E. J. Ward, editor; New York: D. Appleton and Company, 1913, pp. 328-337.

Expert Survey of Public School System, Boise, Idaho. Boise: n. p., 1913. (With C. H. Judd and G. D. Strayer)

"A Tentative Scale for Measuring Teacher Efficiency," *The Supervision of City Schools, 12th Yearbook of the Society for the Study of Education, Part I.* Chicago: University of Chicago Press, 1913.

1914 —
"The New Conscience and the Old Confidence," *Proceedings of the Sixty-first Annual Session of the Wisconsin Teachers Association, 1913.* Madison: Democrat Printing Company, 1914, pp. 46-48.

"Sufficiency and Efficiency of School Control," *Journal of Proceedings and Addresses of the Fifty-first Annual Meeting of the Minnesota Educational Association, October 22-25, 1913.* Minneapolis: Published by the association, 1914, pp. 221-227.

"State School Surveys," *School Board Journal,* 48:9-10, 62, March, 1914.

"Some Whys and Wherefores of School Surveys," *Wisconsin Journal of Education,* 46:131-133, May, 1914.

Report of the Course for the Training of Teachers for the Biennial Period Ending June 30, 1914. (Bulletin of the University of Wisconsin, No. 715, General Series No. 579.) Madison, Wisconsin: Published by the university, 1914.

"The University and Public Service," *Tenth Annual Report of the Canadian Alpine Club of Winnipeg, 1914.* Winnipeg: Published by the club, 1914, pp. 21-22.

"A Plan for Cooperation Between States for the Placing and Promotion of Experienced and Meritorious Teachers," *The School Review Monographs, No. V,* National Society of College Teachers of Education. Chicago: University of Chicago Press, 1914, pp. 37-40.

A Study of Education in Vermont. (The Carnegie Foundation for the Advancement of Teaching, Bulletin No. 7.) New York: The Carnegie Foundation for the Advancement of Teaching, 1914. (With M. B. Hillegas, W. S. Learned and others)

Provisional Plan for the Measurement of Merit of Teachers. Madison, Wisconsin: Democrat Printing Company, 1914.

City School Supervision. Yonkers-on-Hudson, New York: World Book Company, 1914.

1915 —
"Rural School Administration," *School and Society,* 1:154-161, January 30, 1915. (With Ellwood P. Cubberley)

"How Shall the Efficiency of Teachers Be Tested and Recorded," *Proceedings of the Department of Superintendence of the National Education Association, February, 1915.* Washington, D. C.: Government Printing Office, 1915, pp. 217-221.

"Census and Attendance," and "Records and Reports," *The Portland Survey.* Ellwood P. Cubberley, editor; Yonkers-on-Hudson, New York: World Book Company, 1915, pp. 375-403.

State and County School Administration, Vol. II, Source Book. New York: The Macmillan Company, 1915. (With Ellwood P. Cubberley)

1916 —
"Inaugural Address as Chancellor of the University of Montana," *University of Montana Bulletin* (General Series, No. 1.) Helena, Montana: Published by the University, 1916.

"Greetings on Behalf of the Universities of the West," (unpublished address delivered at Inaugural Exercises, University of Washington, Seattle, March 20, 1916).

"The Banks and the University," *Proceedings, Thirteenth Annual Convention, Montana State Bankers Association, 1916.* Miles City, Montana: Published by the association, 1916, pp. 87-98.

1917 —

"Administrative Responsibility and Current Doctrines of Academic Freedom," *School and Society,* 6:1-3, August, 1917.

1919 —

"Higher Education," *Addresses and Proceedings of the National Education Association, 1919.* Washington, D. C.: Government Printing Office, 1919, pp. 73-75.

1921 —

"Universities and Colleges of the West," (unpublished address delivered at a banquet in connection with inaugural exercises, Yale University, New Haven, June 21, 1921).

"The Ranking of Montana's Educational System," *Educational Review,* 62:91-97, September, 1921.

1922 —

"Preliminary Proposals—Purdue University," (unpublished paper presented at the meeting of the Board of Trustees, Purdue University, Lafayette, Indiana, May 16, 1922).

"Message to the Alumni," *The Purdue Alumnus,* 9:6, June, 1922.

"Letter to the Alumni of the Institutions of the University of Montana," *University of Montana Bulletin, Alumni Series,* 6:3-4, July, 1922.

"Letter of Resignation as Chancellor of the University of Montana," *University of Montana Bulletin, Alumni Series,* 6:7-8, July, 1922.

"Foreword," *The Purdue Alumnus,* 10:1, October, 1922.

1923 —

"The University and the Legislature," *The Purdue Alumnus,* 10:9, March, 1923.

"Prexies Invitation," *The Purdue Alumnus,* 10:9, June, 1923.

"The President's Review of the Year 1922-1923," *Bulletin of Purdue University,* 24:5-7, December, 1923.

1924 —

"The Work of the Educational Finance Inquiry," *The Educational Record,* 5:56-66, January, 1924.

"An Old Message and a New Year," *The Purdue Alumnus,* 11:1, January, 1924.

"Statement Re: Semi-Centennial Celebration," *The Purdue Alumnus,* 11:2, 4, February, 1924.

"Alumni-Alluminite," *The Purdue Alumnus,* 11:3, May, 1924.

"Gala Week Impressions," *The Purdue Alumnus,* 11:16, July, 1924.

"To the Faithful Ones," *The Purdue Alumnus,* 12:7, October, 1924.

"The President's Review of the Year 1923-1924," *Bulletin of Purdue University,* 25:12-16, December, 1924.

"President's Preface," *Semi-Centennial Alumni Record, Vol. 24, No. 7.* Lafayette: Published by Purdue University, 1924, p. 4.

1925 —

"Legislative 'Economy' Prunes Purdue Requests," *The Purdue Alumnus,* 12:3, 11, March, 1925.

"Introduction," *Pharmaceutical Views and Activities,* published by Purdue University, Vol. XXV, Bulletin No. 9, May, 1925.

"The President's Review of the Year 1924-1925," *Bulletin of Purdue University,* 26:25-28, December, 1925.

"Progress in Colleges and Universities," *Journal of Proceedings and Addresses of the Sixty-third Annual Meeting of the National Education Association of the United States.* Washington, D. C.: Government Printing Office, 1925, pp. 32-37.

Unit Costs of Higher Education. New York: The Macmillan Company, 1924. (With E. B. Stevens)

1926 —

"What's at the End of the Road?" *Municipal and County Engineering,* 70:183-184, March, 1926.

"Who Should Pay the Costs of Higher Education?" *Minutes of the Seventh Annual Meeting of the Association of University and College Business Officers of the Eastern States, Princeton University, November 18-20, 1926.* —:—, 1926.

"Some Problems in Education," *Proceedings, American Association of Junior Colleges, Jackson, Mississippi, November, 1926,* —:—, 1926, pp. 70-75.

"An Address before the Indiana Farm Bureau Federation," *The Hoosier Farmer,* —:14, December 15, 1926.

"Purdue University and Its Service to Indiana," *Proceedings of Industrial Conference.* (Engineering Extension Department, Bulletin No. 15.) Lafayette: published by Purdue University, 1926, pp. 25-38.

"Discussion of 'The Problem of the Separated State University and the Separated Land Grant College in the Same State'," *Proceedings of the 40th Annual Convention of the Association of Land Grant Colleges and Universities, 1926.* Washington: —, 1926, pp. 26-29.

1927 —

"The President's Review of the Year 1925-1926," *Bulletin of Purdue University,* 27:12-18, March, 1927.

"Signed and Countersigned," *The Purdue Alumnus,* 14:5, April, 1927.

1928 —

"The Purdue Semi-Centennial," *Addresses and Records, Semi-Centennial Ceremonial, Purdue University, May, 1924.* R. W. Babcock, editor; Lafayette: Published by Purdue University, 1928, pp. 3-4.

"The Pursuit of Power," *Addresses and Records, Semi-Centennial Ceremonial, Purdue University, May, 1924.* R. W. Babcock, editor; Lafayette: Published by Purdue University, 1928, pp. 81-87.

"Educational Experiments and Publicity," *Problems of College Education.* Earl Hudelson, editor; Minneapolis: University of Minnesota Press, 1928, pp. 37-48.

"The Qualifications of a College President," *Classified Speech Models.* W. N. Brigance, editor; New York: F. S. Crofts and Company, 1928, pp. 305-311.

1929 —

"For the Trustees and the Faculty," *Thomas Francis Moran. A Memorial, Purdue University, February, 1929.* Lafayette: Published by Purdue University, 1929, pp. 19-20.

"The President's Page," *The Purdue Alumnus,* 17:3, October, 1929.

"The President's Page," *The Purdue Alumnus,* 17:3, November, 1929.

"The President's Page," *The Purdue Alumnus,* 17:3, December, 1929.

"The Memorial of Today and the Union of Tomorrow," *The Memorial Union.* Lafayette: Published by Purdue University, 1929, pp. 19-21.

"The Problems of Articulation as seen by the Colleges and Professional Schools," *Report of the Convention of the Department of Superintendence, National Education Association, 1929.* Washington, D. C.: Government Printing Office, 1929, pp. 683-690.

"The President's Prelude," *Alumni Record and Campus Encyclopedia, Vol. 24, No. 12.* Lafayette: Published by Purdue University, 1929, p. 3.

1930 —

"The President's Page," *The Purdue Alumnus,* 17:3, January, 1930.

"The President's Page," *The Purdue Alumnus,* 17:3, February, 1930.

"The President's Page," *The Purdue Alumnus,* 17:3, March, 1930.

"The President's Page," *The Purdue Alumnus,* 17:3, April, 1930.

"Men, Mentality and Machinery," (unpublished address delivered at Washington State College, May 29, 1930).

"The President's Page," *The Purdue Alumnus,* 17:3, May, 1930.

"The President's Review of the Biennium 1926-1928," *Bulletin of Purdue University,* 30:17-22, May, 1930.

"The President's Review of the Year 1928-1929," *Bulletin of Purdue University,* 30:15-17, May, 1930.

"There are Giants on the Earth in These Days," *Oregon State Agricultural College Bulletin.* No. 467, June, 1930.

"The President's Page," *The Purdue Alumnus,* 17:3, June, 1930.

"The President's Page," *The Purdue Alumnus,* 18:1, October, 1930.

"The President's Page," *The Purdue Alumnus,* 18:1, November, 1930.

"The President's Page," *The Purdue Alumnus,* 18:1, December, 1930.

"The Board of Control," *Higher Education in America.* R. A. Kent, editor; Boston: Ginn and Company, 1930, pp. 600-632.

1931 —

"The President's Page," *The Purdue Alumnus,* 18:1, January, 1931.

"The President's Page," *The Purdue Alumnus,* 18:1, February, 1931.

"The President's Page," *The Purdue Alumnus,* 18:1, March, 1931.

"The President's Review of the Year 1929-1930," *Bulletin of Purdue University,* 31:15-21, March, 1931.

"The Years and the Yearnings," (unpublished dedication address delivered at North Platte High School, North Platte, Nebraska, March, 13, 1931).

"The President's Page," *The Purdue Alumnus,* 18:1, April, 1931.

"The President's Page," *The Purdue Alumnus,* 18:1, May, 1931.

"The President's Page," *The Purdue Alumnus,* 18:1, June, 1931.

"The National Advisory Committee on Education," *The North Central Association Quarterly,* 6:160-164, September, 1931.

"The President's Page," *The Purdue Alumnus,* 19:3, October, 1931.

"The President's Page," *The Purdue Alumnus,* 19:3, November, 1931.

"The President's Review of the Year 1930-1931," *Bulletin of Purdue University,* 32:15-23, November, 1931.

"A Memory—Thomas A. Edison," *The Purdue Engineer,* 27:1, November, 1931.

"Thomas Duncan—Benefactor," *The Purdue Engineer,* 27:60-62, December, 1931.

"The President's Page," *The Purdue Alumnus,* 19:3, December, 1931.

"The President's Letter," *Purdue Research Foundation Bulletin No. 1.* Lafayette: Purdue University, 1931, p. 8.

"Progress Report of Activities Since the First Industrial Conference of June 1, 1926," *Purdue Research Foundation Bulletin No. 2.* Lafayette: Published by Purdue University, 1931, pp. 20-31, 65-66.

1932 —

"The President's Page," *The Purdue Alumnus,* 19:3, January, 1932.

"Purdue and You," *The Purdue Alumnus,* 19:8, January, 1932.

"The President's Page," *The Purdue Alumnus,* 19:3, February, 1932.

"The President's Page," *The Purdue Alumnus,* 19:3, March, 1932.

"The President's Page," *The Purdue Alumnus,* 19:3, April, 1932.

"The President's Page," *The Purdue Alumnus,* 19:3, May, 1932.

"The President's Page," *The Purdue Alumnus,* 19:3, June, 1932.

"The President's Page," *The Purdue Alumnus,* 20:3, October, 1932.

"In Defense of R.O.T.C. Organizations," *The Purdue Alumnus,* 20:13-14, October, 1932.

"The President's Page," *The Purdue Alumnus,* 20:3, November, 1932.

"The President's Page," *The Purdue Alumnus,* 20:3, December, 1932.

Report to the Board of Regents of the University System of Georgia. Atlanta: Published by the University of Georgia, 1932. (With L. D. Coffman, C. H. Judd, G. F. Zook, and G. A. Works)

"Dollars for Ideals: Ideals for Dividends," *Purdue Research Foundation Bulletin No. 3.* Lafayette: Published by Purdue University, 1932, pp. 27-37.

"Statement Concerning Ellwood P. Cubberley," *The Cubberley Booklet.* Palo Alto: Stanford University, 1932.

1933 —

"The President's Page," *The Purdue Alumnus,* 20:3, January, 1933.

"The President's Page," *The Purdue Alumnus,* 20:3, February, 1933.

"The President's Page," *The Purdue Alumnus,* 20:3, March, 1933.

"The President's Page," *The Purdue Alumnus,* 20:3, April, 1933.

"The President's Page," *The Purdue Alumnus,* 20:3, May, 1933.

"The President's Page," *The Purdue Alumnus,* 20:3, June, 1933.

"President Elliott's Page," *The Purdue Alumnus,* 21:3, October, 1933.

"President Elliott's Page," *The Purdue Alumnus,* 21:3, November, 1933.

"President Elliott's Page," *The Purdue Alumnus,* 21:3, December, 1933.

"The Value of Technical Training for Young Men, and Their Future in Transportation Work," *Official Proceedings, The Western Railway Club,* 46:11-18, December, 1933.

"Report of Committee 'D' on Free Schooling at Higher Levels," *Proceedings, Citizens Conference on the Crisis in Education, 1933.* Washington, D. C.: American Council on Education, 1933, pp. 48-50. (With T. N. McCarter and Spence Miller)

"Letter of Transmittal," *Purdue University, 1922-1932.* R. W. Babcock, editor; Lafayette: Published by Purdue University, 1933, p. v.

"Preface," *Purdue University, 1922-1932.* R. W. Babcock, editor; Lafayette: Purdue University, 1933, pp. vii-ix.

1934 —

"President Elliott's Page," *The Purdue Alumnus,* 21:3, January, 1934.

"President Elliott's Page," *The Purdue Alumnus,* 21:3, February, 1934.

"What Can We Do to Aid the Student Affected by the Depression," *Journal of Engineering Education.* 24:383-387, February, 1934.

"President Elliott's Page," *The Purdue Alumnus,* 21:3, March, 1934.

"President Elliott's Page," *The Purdue Alumnus,* 21:3, April, 1934.

"The President's Review of the Biennium 1931-1933," *Bulletin of Purdue University,* 34:15-21, April, 1934.

"President Elliott's Page," *The Purdue Alumnus,* 21:3, May, 1934.

"President Elliott's Page," *The Purdue Alumnus,* 21:3, June, 1934.

"Special Purdue Editorial," *The Purdue Alumnus,* 22:3, October, 1934.

Charters and Basic Laws of Selected American Universities and Colleges. New York: The Carnegie Foundation for the Advancement of Teaching, 1934. (With M. M. Chambers)

"New Frontiers for Youth," *Changing Standards, Report of the Fourth Annual Women's Conference on Current Problems.* New York: New York Herald Tribune, 1934, pp. 125-131.

"The President's Foreword," *Alumni Directory 1875-1934.* Lafayette: Published by Purdue University, 1934, p. iv.

1935 —

"The President's Review of the Year 1933-1934," *Bulletin of Purdue University,* 35:15-21, January, 1935.

"Appreciation and Anticipation," *The Purdue Alumnus,* 22:3, June, 1935.

"New Firsts," *The Purdue Alumnus,* 23:2, October, 1935.

"Purdue Research Foundation Accepts Challenge," *The Purdue Alumnus,* 23:4-5, 22-23, October, 1935.

"Three Tributes," *Proceedings of the Association of Governing Boards of State Universities and Allied Institutions, November 7-9, 1935.* Lincoln: University of Nebraska, 1935, pp. 43-47.

"Out of the House of the University into the Home of the People," *Purdue Research Foundation Bulletin No. 6.* Lafayette: Published by Purdue University, 1935, pp. 33-45.

The Government of Higher Education. New York: American Book Company, 1935. (With M. M. Chambers and W. A. Ashbrook)

"Memorandum," *Progress Report of the Ross Ade Foundation.* Lafayette: Published by Purdue University, 1935, pp. 1, 5.

"John Purdue," *Dictionary of American Biography, Vol. 15.* New York: Charles Scribner's Sons, 1935, p. 268.

Occupational Opportunities and the Economic Status of Recent Graduates (1928-1934) of Purdue University. Lafayette: Published by Purdue University, 1935. (With Frank C. Hockema and Jack E. Walters)

1936 —

"The President's Review of the Sixty-first Year of the University (1934-1935)," *Bulletin of Purdue University,* 36:15-22, January, 1936.

"The Day and the Dust," *Nebraska Alumnus,* 32:4-5, 24, 26, March, 1936.

"Economic Importance of Scientific Education," *Proceedings of the Second Dearborn Conference, May 12-14, 1936.* New York: The Farm Chemurgic Council (Dearborn, Michigan) and the Chemical Foundation, Incorporated, 1936, pp. 15-17.

"Vocational Education for Adults in a Changing Economic Order," *Journal of Adult Education,* 8:343-344, June, 1936.

"The Purdue University Fieldhouse and Gymnasium for Men," *The Purdue Alumnus,* 23:7-8, June, 1936.

"Busy as Ever," *The Purdue Alumnus,* 24:2, October, 1936.

Where They Go and What They Do, A Report Upon the Graduates of Purdue University. Lafayette: Published by Purdue University, 1936. (With Frank C. Hockema)

The Colleges and the Courts. New York: The Carnegie Foundation for the Advancement of Teaching, 1936. (With M. M. Chambers)

"The Scientific Hunt for Sensible Housing," *Report of the Sixth Annual New York* Herald Tribune *Forum on Current Problems on "The New Way of Living" and "The Political Issues Which America Faces in 1936."* New York: New York *Herald Tribune,* 1936, pp. 53-60.

Higher Education in the State of New York. New York: Published by the Regents' Inquiry into the Character and Cost of Public Education in the State of New York, 1936.

1937 —

"The President's Review of the Sixty-second Year of the University (1935-1936)," *Bulletin of Purdue University,* 37:19-24, February, 1937.

"The Two-Sided Head," *The Peabody Reflector and Alumni News,* 10:205-206, June, 1937.

"Tribute to Amelia Earhart," (unpublished address delivered at the Conference on Women's Work and Opportunities, Purdue University, October 21, 1937).

"As Usual," *The Purdue Alumnus,* 25:2, October, 1937.

"Remarks Made in Presenting Log, Charts, and Maps of the Last Flight of Amelia Earhart," (unpublished address delivered at the Inauguration Dinner, The World Center for Women's Archives, New York City, December 15, 1937).

The University in Action. Vol. II. The Rise of a University, 2 vols. New York: Columbia University Press, 1937.

Higher Education in the State of New York. New York: published by the Regents' Inquiry into the Character and Cost of Public Education in the State of New York, 1937. (With David S. Hill)

"The Interdependence of Science and Technology," *Technological Trends and National Policy,* Science Committee of the National Resources Committee. Washington, D. C.: United States Government Printing Office, 1937, pp. 93-94.

1938 —

"The Man Beneath the Surface," (unpublished tribute to David E. Ross, January 14, 1938).

"The President's Review of the Sixty-third Year of the University (1936-1937), *Bulletin of Purdue University,* 38:19-30, February, 1938.

"Greetings to President Garrison and Chancellor Carmichael at the Inaugural Ceremonies of Dr. Garrison as President of George Peabody College for Teachers and Dr. Carmichael as Chancellor of Vanderbilt University," *The Peabody Reflector and Alumni News,* 11:86, March, 1938.

"Tactics and Techniques," (unpublished commencement address delivered at Chrysler Institute of Engineering, Detroit, Michigan, June 14, 1938).

"Counsel for the Council," *The Educational Record,* 19:304-311, July, 1938.

"New September," *The Purdue Alumnus,* 26:2, October, 1938.

"Letter to Frank C. Hockema," *The Purdue Alumnus,* 26:2, —, 1938.

"Preface," *Adult Education,* by F. W. Reeves, T. Fansler, and C. O. Houle. New York: The McGraw-Hill Book Company, Inc., 1938, pp. xi-xiii.

1939 —

"Feels Great to be Back on the Campus," *The Purdue Alumnus,* 26:2-3, February, 1939.

"The President's Review of the Sixty-fourth Year of the University (1937-1938)," *Bulletin of Purdue University,* 39:19-37, February, 1939.

"Founder's Day Address," *The Purdue Alumnus,* 26:5, May, 1939.

"Proving and Improving Teaching," *Bulletin of the President's Committee on the Improvement of Teaching,* University of the Philippines, 5:1-11, August, 1939.

"Remarks at the Dedication of Sculpture at the Union Entrance," *The Purdue Alumnus,* 27:5-6, November, 1939.

"Purdue Philosophy," *The Purdue Alumnus,* 27:3, December, 1939.

Summary Memorandum with Reference to Higher Education. New York: published by the Regents' Inquiry into the Character and Cost of Public Education in the State of New York, 1939.

Charters of Philanthropies. New York: The Carnegie Foundation for the Advancement of Teaching in co-operation with Purdue University, 1939. (With M. M. Chambers)

"Memoranda of Education Advisers," *Report on a Survey of the University of the Philippines.* Manila: University of the Philippines, 1939, pp. 161-286. (With Paul C. Packer)

1940 —

"The President's Review of the Sixty-fifty Year of the University (1938-1939)," *Bulletin of Purdue University,* 40:21-38, January, 1940.

"Remarks at the Dedication of the Hall of Music, May 3-4, 1940," *The Commencement Season.* Lafayette: Published by Purdue University, 1940, pp. 14, 19.

"Remarks at the Conferring of the Honorary Degree of Doctor of Humane Letters upon Booth Tarkington, May 7, 1940," *The Commencement Season.* Lafayette: Published by Purdue University, 1940, p. 63.

"Address to the Class of 1940, June 9, 1940," *The Commencement Season.* Lafayette: Published by Purdue University, 1940, pp. 73-74.

"1951—The Effect of the Next Ten Years on Education," *The University of Chicago Round Table.* 146:2-19, December 29, 1940.

"The Archives Preface," *The Trustees and the Officers of Purdue University 1865-1940, The Archives of Purdue, No. 1.* Lafayette: Published by Purdue University, 1940, pp. 9-11.

"Tribute to Stanley Coulter," *The Dean,* by John G. Coulter. Lafayette: Published by the Haywood Publishing Co., 1940, p. 235.

"Introduction," *Wanted: A JOB!* Washington: American Council on Education, 1940.

"An Address in Honor of the Honorable Chase S. Osborn," *An Accolade for Chase S. Osborn.* Stella Brunt Osborn, editor; Sault St. Marie, Michigan: Published by the City of Sault St. Marie, 1940, pp. 70-75.

"Report on Regional Cooperation," *Proceedings of the Association of Governing Boards of State Universities and Allied Institutions, 1940.* Bloomington, Indiana: The Association of Governing Boards of State Universities and Allied Institutions, 1940, pp. 87-92.

"The Functions and Relations of a College President and His Governing Board," *Proceedings of the Association of Governing Boards of State Universities and Allied Institutions, 1940.* Bloomington, Indiana: The Association of Governing Boards of State Universities and Allied Institutions, 1940, pp. 93-100.

1941 —

"The President's Review of the Sixty-sixth Year of the University (1939-1940)," *Bulletin of Purdue University,* 41:23-41, January, 1941.

"Democracy and the Land Grant Colleges," *The Nation's Agriculture,* 16:10, 30, January, 1941.

"The Power of Purdue University," *Program for Vim-Vision-Victory Convocation, September 10, 1941.* Lafayette: Published by Purdue University, 1941.

The Day and Our Duties. Lafayette: Published by Purdue University, 1941.

"Commentary and Afterthought," *American Council on Education Studies, Series I, Vol. V. No. 13.* Washington, D.C.: American Council on Education, 1941, pp. 64-67.

"Foreword," *The Colleges and The Courts 1936-1940,* by M. M. Chambers. New York: The Carnegie Foundation for the Advancement of Teaching, 1941, pp. v-vi.

"For the Association of Land-Grant Colleges and Universities," *History of the Ohio State University, Vol. V.* William McPherson and Harold Kent Schellenger, editors; Columbus: Ohio State University Press, 1941, pp. 65-67.

1942 —

"The President's Review of the Sixty-seventh Year of the University (1940-1941)," *Bulletin of Purdue University,* 42:23-45, January, 1942.

"Statement of Edward C. Elliott, President, Purdue University, Lafayette, Indiana," *Termination of Civilian Conservation Corps and National Youth Administration, Hearings before the Committee on Education and Labor, United States Senate, Seventy-seventh Congress, on S.2295, March 23 to April 17, 1942.* Washington, D. C.: Government Printing Office, 1942, pp. 128-143.

"In Memoriam," *The Purdue Alumnus,* 29:4, April, 1942.

"Country Land-Use Planning for Better Agriculture," *American Planning and Civic Annual.* Washington, D. C.: American Planning and Civic Association, 1942, pp. 167-173.

"Will to Win With Manpower," *A Record of the Program of a Will-to-win Convocation held at Purdue University, September 2, 1942.* Lafayette: Published by the University, 1942, pp. 5-7.

"Statement of Dr. E. C. Elliott, President of Purdue University, Chief of the Division of Professional and Technical Employment and Training of the War Manpower Commission," *Lowering Draft Age to 18 Years, Hearings Before the Committee on Military Affairs, House of Representatives, Seventy-seventh Congress, on H. R. 7528, October 14-15, 1942.* Washington, D. C.: Government Printing Office, 1942.

"A Concluding Discussion," *College Women and the War, Northwestern University Information,* 11:20-21, November 9, 1942.

"Purdue University," *Purdue Alumnus,* 30:4, December, 1942.

"The High Schools and the Problems of Manpower," *Studies in Higher Education, Vol. 47.* Lafayette: Published by Purdue University, 1942, pp. 36-40.

A Prologue to Service. Lafayette: Published by Purdue University, 1942.

"Tribute to Dean Jordan," *A Book of Tributes to Charles Bernard Jordan, Dean of Pharmacy, 1910-1941.* Lafayette: Published by Purdue University, 1942, p. 4.

"The Utilization of the Facilities of the Land-Grant Colleges and Universities," *Proceedings of the Association of Land-Grant Colleges and Universities*. Chicago: Association of Land-Grant Colleges and Universities, 1942, pp. 47-54.

"How Shall the Colleges and Universities Assist the Army, Navy, and the War Manpower Commission in Their Student Recruitment and Training Program?" *Proceedings of the National Institute on Education and the War*. Washington, D.C.: Government Printing Office, 1942.

"Memorandum Relative to the Committee on Resolutions and Recommendations," *Higher Education and the War, American Council on Education Studies, Series I, Vol. VI, No. 16*. Washington, D. C.: American Council on Education, 1942, p. 152.

1943 —

"The President's Review of the Sixty-eighth Year of the University (1941-1942)," *Bulletin of Purdue University*, 43:17-20, January, 1943.

"Statement of Dr. Edward C. Elliott, Director of the Educational Program of the War Manpower Commission, and President of Purdue University," *Inquiry into Army and Navy Educational Program, Hearings before the Committee on Military Affairs, House of Representatives, Seventy-eighth Congress, February, 9, 16, 1943*. Washington, D. C.: Government Printing Office, 1943.

"Education and the War," *The Journal of the American Medical Association*, 121:631-633, February 27, 1943.

"To the High School Graduate," *The Purdue Alumnus*, 30:13, March-April, 1943.

"Postwar Needs for Medical and Other Trained Personnel," *The Journal of the American Medical Association*, 122:18-20, May, 1943.

"Demobilization and Readjustment," *Report of the Conference on Postwar Readjustment of Civilian and Military Personnel*. Washington, D. C.: The National Resources Planning Board, June, 1943.

"Convocation Address," *The Purdue Alumnus*, 30:2-3, September, 1943.

"The Cracking of Wisdom," (unpublished commencement address delivered at the University of Pittsburgh, Pittsburgh, Pennsylvania, September 17, 1943).

The Job of Jobs. Endicott, N. Y.: IBM Department of Education, December 16, 1943.

"The Selection of Institutions for Specialized Training Programs," *Proceedings of the Institute for Administrative Officers of Higher Institutions, Vol. XV*. Chicago: The University of Chicago, 1943, pp. 63-73.

"Selected Current Problems of American Higher Education," *Proceedings of the Eighth American Scientific Congress, Vol. XII, Education*. Washington, D. C.: Department of State, 1943, pp. 17-22.

1944 —

"Whither—When and Why," *The North Central Association Quarterly*, 18:216-224, January, 1944.

"Statement of Dr. Edward C. Elliott, President, Purdue University, Lafayette, Indiana," *Extending the Civilian Pilot Training Act of 1939, Hearing Before a Subcommittee of the Committee on Commerce, United States Senate, Seventy-eighth Congress, on S. 1932, February 2-3, 1944*. Washington, D. C.: Government Printing Office, 1944.

"A Tribute to James W. Noel," *The Purdue Alumnus*, 31:9, March-April, 1944.

"The President's Letter," *Purdue Research Foundation Bulletin No. 1*. Lafayette: Purdue University, Revised May, 1944. P. 5.

"A Final Tribute to Purdue University's 'Walking Delegate'," *The Magazine of Sigma Chi*, 63:77-80, October-November, 1944.

1945 —

"An Educator Looks at UMT," *The American Legion Magazine*, 38:19, 46-47, April, 1945.

"Should We Have Universal Military Training After the War?" *Bulletin of America's Town Meeting of the Air, Vol. 2*, July 5, 1945. Columbus, Ohio: The Reader's Digest, 1945.

"Higher Education in West Virginia—The University," *A Digest of a Report of a Survey of Public Education in the State of West Virginia*, by George D. Strayer. Legislative Interim Committee, State of West Virginia, 1945, pp. 117-127.

1946 —

"Does Atomic Warfare Make Universal Military Training Obsolete? The *American Forum of the Air, Vol. 8, February 12, 1946*. Washington, D. C.: Ransdell, Inc., 1946.

"The Pharmacy Survey—For What and For Whom," *Report of Annual Meeting, National Wholesale Druggist Association, Atlantic City, September 25, 1946*. ———: Published by the Association, 1946, pp. 18-24.

"Answers Versus The Questions," *Journal of the American Pharmaceutical Association*, 7:450-453, October, 1946.

"Trivia From Oblivia," *Journal of Engineering Education*, 37:260-267, November, 1946.

"Survey of Pharmaceutical Education in the United States," *The American Journal of Pharmaceutical Education*, 10:265, —, 1946. 1946.

"The Professional as a Person," *American Journal of Pharmaceutical Education*, 10:442-448, —, 1946.

"The Way of the Pharmaceutical Survey," *American Journal of Pharmaceutical Education*, 10:449-457, —, 1946.

"Pharmaceutical Survey—Report on Progress," *The American Journal of Pharmaceutical Education*, 10:672, —, 1946.

"Foreword," *The Colleges and The Courts, 1941-1945*, by M. M. Chambers. New York: The Carnegie Foundation for the Advancement of Teaching, 1946, pp. v-vi.

1947 —

"Charles Hubbard Judd—1873-1946," *The Educational Forum* 11:256h-256i, January, 1947.

"Should Congress Adopt Universal Military Training?" *The American Forum of the Air, Vol. 9, November 11, 1947.* Washington: Ransdell, Inc., 1947.

"The Decade of Destiny for Pharmacy," *National Association of Retail Druggists Journal,* 69:2158-2159, November 17, 1947.

"Pharmaceutical Survey—Report on Progress," *The American Journal of Pharmaceutical Education,* 11:337, —, 1947.

"Pharmaceutical Survey Current," *The American Journal of Pharmaceutical Education,* 11:190, 194, 590, 857, —, 1947.

"The Effective Board of Control," *The Administration of Higher Institutions Under Changing Conditions,* Norman Burns, editor. Proceedings of the Institute for Administrative Officers of Higher Institutions, Vol. XIX, 1947. Chicago: The University of Chicago Press, 1947, pp. 20-26.

1948 —

"A Fifty-Year Program?" *The Journal of Higher Education,* 19:175-180, April, 1948.

"Beginnings of the End," *Journal of the American Pharmaceutical Association,* 9:550-555, September, 1948.

"Eyeing the Future of Instruction for the Profession of Pharmacy," *The American Journal of Pharmaceutical Education,* 12:666ff, —, 1948.

"Spearheading the Progress and Protection of the Profession of Pharmacy," *The American Journal of Pharmaceutical Education,* 12:698ff, —, 1948.

"The Pharmaceutical Survey—The Beginnings of the End," *The American Journal of Pharmaceutical Education,* 12:708ff, —, 1948.

"I Remember Du Mez," *The American Journal of Pharmaceutical Education,* 12:870ff, —, 1948.

"The Effects of Wartime Research Upon Institutions of Higher Learning," *Wartime College Training Programs of the Armed Services,* By Henry C. Herge and others. Washington, D. C.: American Council on Education, 1948, pp. 178-207.

"Foreword," *Charters of Philanthropies,* by M. M. Chambers. New York: The Carnegie Foundation for the Advancement of Teaching, 1948, p. v.

1949 —

"Pharmacy Takes a New Look at Itself," *Higher Education,* 5:137-139, February 15, 1949.

"Recent Adventures in Accreditation," *American Journal of Pharmaceutical Education,* 13:253-262, April, 1949.

"Implementation is Not Automatic," *American Journal of Pharmaceutical Education,* 13:263-270, April, 1949.

1950 —

"Recent Steps Toward Coordination and Improvement of Accrediting Procedures," *American Journal of Pharmaceutical Education,* 14:158-162, January, 1950.

"Actions and Reactions on the Survey Recommendations," *American Journal of Pharmaceutical Education,* 14:400-405, July, 1950.

The General Report of the Pharmaceutical Survey, 1946-1949. Washington: American Council on Education, 1950.

1951 —

"Prescript," *Cumulative Index of the American Journal of Pharmaceutical Education,* Volumes 1-13, 1937-1949, by H. W. Youngken, Jr., and J. M. Dille. Washington, D. C.: American Council on Education, 1951, p. 4.

1952 —

"A Pharmaceutical Postscript," *The Indiana Pharmacist,* 34:177-178, June, 1952.
"Foreword—The Pharmaceutical Survey," *The Pharmaceutical Curriculum,* by Lloyd E. Blauch and George L. Webster. Washington, D. C.: American Council on Education, 1952, pp. vii-ix.
"Foreword," *The Colleges and The Courts, 1946-1950,* by M. M. Chambers. New York: Columbia University Press, 1952.

1954 —

"Note for The Purdue Pharmacist in Recognition of Professor Charles O. Lee," *The Purdue Pharmacist,* 31:6, April, 1954.

1955 —

"Between Ourselves—Old Notes and New Counter Notes," *The American Journal of Pharmaceutical Education,* 19:633-645, Fall, 1955.

1957 —

"A Tribute to Samuel Paul Capen," *The Educational Record,* 38:18-19, January, 1957.

INDEX

Photographs for this book were provided by the Elliott family and by the Purdue University Libraries, Photographic Service, and News Service. The book was printed in Baskerville and Caslon typefaces on 60 lb. Warren Olde Style paper, with 60 lb. Production Gloss used for the two photo sections. Printing was done by C. E. Pauley and Company, Indianapolis, Indiana, and the H & H Bookbinding Company, Indianapolis, bound the books. The dust jacket was designed by Dan Estes and editorial and production supervision were by Diane Dubiel, assistant university editor.